Authentic Recipes from the
PHILIPPINES

Recipes by Reynaldo G. Alejandro

Introductory essays by Doreen G. Fernandez, Corazon S. Alvina and Millie Reyes

Photographs by Luca Invernizzi Tettoni

PERIPLUS

Published by Periplus Editions, with editorial offices at
130 Joo Seng Road #06-01, Singapore 368357.
Tel: (65) 6280-1330; fax: (65) 6280-6290.
Email: inquiries@periplus.com.sg
Website: www.periplus.com

Hardcover ISBN: 0-7946-0238-X
Paperback ISBN: 0-7946-0286-X
Printed in Singapore

Distributed by

North America, Latin America and Europe

Tuttle Publishing, 364 Innovation Drive,
North Clarendon, VT 05759-9436,
Tel: (802) 773-8930; fax: (802) 773-6993.
Email: info@tuttlepublishing.com

Japan and Korea

Tuttle Publishing, Yaekari Building 3F,
5-4-12 Osaki, Shinagawa-ku, Tokyo 141-0032.
Tel: (03) 5437-0171; fax: (03) 5437-0755.
Email: tuttle-sales@gol.com

Asia Pacific

Berkeley Books Pte Ltd
130 Joo Seng Road #06-01, Singapore 368357.
Tel: (65) 6280-1330; fax: (65) 6280-6290.
Email: inquiries@periplus.com.sg
Website: www.periplus.com

All recipes were tested in the Periplus Test Kitchen

Photo credits: Food photography by Luca Invernizzi
Tettoni. Additional photos on pages 4, 6, 9, 13 from
Photobank Singapore; pages 7, 8, 10–12 and 14 by
Sonny Yabao. Fiesta print on page 5 reproduced
courtesy of the Gallery of Prints in Manila.

Contents

Food in the Philippines

Islands with a history of colonization nourished a people with a gift for adaptation

by Doreen G. Fernandez

What is Filipino food? Is it *adobo*—which has a Spanish name, yet contains chicken, pork, vegetables or even seafood stewed in vinegar and garlic, and is thus unlike any Spanish *adobado*? Or is it *pancit*—noodles of many persuasions utilizing local ingredients, yet obviously of Chinese origin? Or would it be *sinigang*—the sour broth related to similar Southeast Asian soups and stews that are cooling in the hot tropical weather? Could it even be the omnipresent fried chicken—sometimes marinated in vinegar and garlic before it is fried? Or *arroz caldo*—a chicken congee that is served as comfort food even on airlines?

The land and the waters provide the Filipinos with an abundance of tasty and nutritious food ingredients. Seven thousand and more islands are surrounded by seas, watered by rivers and brooks, bordered by swamps and dotted with lakes, canals, ponds and lagoons, providing a multitude of fish and other water creatures that make up the basic diet of Filipinos. This variegated landscape of mountains and plains, shores and forests, fields and hills is inhabited by land and air creatures that generously transform into food. It also brings forth greenery all year-round, a garden of edible grains, leaves, roots, fruits, pods, seeds, tendrils and flowers.

Thus, the Filipino dietary pattern: rice as the staple, steamed white and plain, providing a background to the flavors of fish, meat and vegetables. It is, nutritionists judge, one of the healthiest eating patterns in the world.

Because the island geography makes food readily accessible to hunters, fishermen, food gatherers and farmers, indigenous dishes are simply prepared: grilled (*ini-haw*), steamed (*pinasingawan*) or boiled (*nilaga*). Some dishes even require no cooking at all, as with *kinilaw*, fish briefly marinated in vinegar or lime juice to "cook" it, while retaining freshness and translucence.

Since food is one of the liveliest areas of popular cultural exchange, it has of course been subject to foreign influences and change. Chinese traders, the Spanish colonizers and proselytizers, and in the 20th century, the United States—all left their mark on the local cuisine. The signature ingre-

dients of Southeast Asia are present here too, in the form of chilies, lemongrass and the pungent fish sauce called *patis*. Recent times have seen foods from other more distant lands sometimes occupying a small corner of the Filipino table. To the question therefore, "What is Filipino food?" One can simply answer, "All of the above."

The Philippines national culture begins with a tropical clime divided into rainy and dry seasons and an archipelago with 7,000 islands. These isles contain the Cordillera mountains, Luzon's central plains, Palawan's coral reefs; seas touching the longest coastline of any nation of comparable area in the world; and a multitude of lakes, rivers, springs and brooks.

The population—120 different ethnic groups and the mainstream communities of Tagalog/Ilocano/ Pampango/ Pangasinan and Visayan lowlanders— developed within a gentle but lush environment. Each group shaped their own lifeways: building houses, weaving cloth, telling and writing stories; ornamenting and decorating, and preparing food.

Foreign influences made a deep impression on native island cultures. Chinese traders who had been coming to the islands since the 11th century brought silks and ceramics, took back products from the forest and sea, and left behind them many traditions so deeply embedded in daily life that Filipinos do not realize their provenance. Filipinos of Chinese ancestry comprise an important facet of the national profile.

In the 16th century, the Spanish colonizers imported Christianity and a dominant Iberian elite that lasted three centuries. Families were "brought within the sound of church bells"; and thus were created villages, towns and cities.

OPPOSITE: Stuffed Crab and Boiled Shrimp. The Filipinos took to the Spanish technique of *rellenado* or "stuffing" with relish.
ABOVE: *"Fête à Santa-Cruz de Nano"*, (1887) by Marcelle Lancelot (after Andrews). First published in *LuCon et Palaouan: Six Années de Voyage aux Philippines* by Alfred Marché. This engraving depicts Manileno *ilustra-dos* enjoying a neighborhood party. *Ilustrados*, meaning "enlightened ones", comprised an elite urban class with a high level of education and nationalism.

Spanish cultural forms replaced or melded with indigenous expressions. The folk cultures of the Christianized lowlands are thus greatly Hispanicized, whereas the highlands were later reached by Protestant missionaries and in southern Mindanao Islam flourished and long resisted Spanish colonization.

After the Revolution of 1889, the Battle of Manila Bay, and the pact of exchange between the US and Spain, the country became an American colony. The US-style government and educational system imported along with the popular culture made Filipinos the most "Americanized Asians", and the Philippines became one of the larger English-speaking countries of the world.

This storied history and Mother Nature's largesse combined and evolved to produce Filipino food.

The Chinese who came to trade sometimes stayed on. Their foodways accompanied them and also stayed. Perhaps they cooked the noodles of home; certainly they used local condiments; surely they taught their Filipino wives their dishes, and thus Filipino-Chinese food came to be. The names identify them: *pancit* (Hokkien for something quickly cooked) are noodles; *lumpia* are vegetables rolled in edible wrappers; *siopao* are steamed, filled buns; *siomai* are dumplings.

All, of course, became indigenized—Filipinized by their ingredients and by local tastes. Today, for example, Pancit

Malabon has oysters and squid, since Malabon is a fishing center; and Pancit Marilao is sprinkled with rice crisps, because Marilao lies within the Luzon rice bowl.

When restaurants were established in the 19th century, Chinese food became a staple of the *pansiterias*, with the food given Spanish names for the ease of the clientele: thus *comida China* (Chinese food) includes *arroz caldo* (rice and chicken gruel); and *morisqueta tostada* (fried rice).

When the Spaniards arrived, the food influences they brought were from both Spain and Mexico, as it was through the vice royalty of Mexico that the Philippines were governed. This meant the production of food for an elite, including many dishes for which ingredients were not locally available.

Spanish Filipino food had new flavors and ingredients—olive oil, paprika, saffron, ham, cheese, cured sausages—and new names. Paella, the dish cooked in the fields by Spanish workers, came to be a festive dish combining pork, chicken, seafood, ham, sausages and vegetables, a luxurious mix of the local and the foreign. Relleno, the process of stuffing festive capons and turkeys for Christmas, was applied to chickens, and even to *bangus*, the silvery milkfish. Christmas, a new feast for Filipinos that coincided with the rice harvest, featured not only the myriad of native rice cakes, but also *ensaymadas* (brioche-like cakes buttered, sugared and sprinkled with cheese) to dip

in hot thick chocolate, and the apples, oranges, chestnuts and walnuts of European Christmases. Even the Mexican corn *tamal* turned Filipino, becoming rice-based *tamales* wrapped in banana leaves.

The Americans introduced to Philippine cuisine the ways of convenience: pressure-cooking, freezing, pre-cooking; sandwiches and salads; hamburgers, fried chicken and steaks. Add to the above other cuisines found in the country along with other global influences: French, Italian, Middle Eastern, Japanese, Thai and Vietnamese. They grow familiar, but remain "imported" and not yet indigenized.

On a buffet table today one might find, for example, Kinilaw Na Tanguingue, mackerel dressed with vinegar, ginger, onions, hot peppers, perhaps coconut milk; also grilled tiger shrimp, and maybe Sinigang Na Baboy, pork and vegetables in a broth soured with tamarind, all from the native repertoire. Alongside there would almost certainly be *pancit*, noodles once Chinese, now Filipino, still in a sweet-sour sauce. Spanish festive fare like Morcon (beef rolls, page 76), Embutido (pork rolls), Fish Escabeche (page 68) and stuffed chicken or turkey might be there too. The centerpiece would probably be Lechon, spit-roasted pig, which may be Chinese or Polynesian in influence, but bears a Spanish name, and may therefore be derived from Cochinillo Asado. Vegetable dishes could include an American salad and a Pinakbet (vegetables

and shrimp paste). The dessert table would surely be richly Spanish: Leche Flan (page 99), Natilla, Yema (page 100), Dulces De Naranja, Membrillo, Torta Del Rey, etc., but also include local fruits in syrup (coconut, *santol*, guavas) and American cakes and pies. The global village may be reflected in *shawarma* and pasta. The buffet table and Filipino food today is thus a gastronomic telling of Philippine history.

What really is Philippine food, then? Indigenous food from land and sea, field and forest. With added dishes and culinary procedures from China, Spain, Mexico and the United States, and more recently from further abroad.

What makes them Filipino? The history and society that introduced and adapted them; the people who tuned them to their tastes and accepted them into their homes and restaurants, and especially the harmonizing culture that combined them into contemporary Filipino fare.

OPPOSITE: Emerald green rice terraces are part of the spectacular scenery in the Cordillera of Northern Philippines.
ABOVE: Fresh food market in Tagaytay, a temperate city located high above Taal Lake in Southern Luzon. Tagaytay is well known for its market gardens and fruit stalls.

Regional Dishes and Regional Identity

In this land of more than 7000 islands, regional diversity is seen and tasted

by Corazon S. Alvina

The Philippine archipelago has conjured a people with a stubborn sense of regional identity. The scattered island geography sustains multiple cultures—and many distinctly different cuisines, all alive and well. Regionalism can be sensed—ay, tasted—on Philippine islanders' taste buds.

While Filipino food comprises essentially a simple, tropical cuisine, diverse styles have evolved among seven major regions of the 7,107 islands. The variations are traceable to the character of, first, the natural resources—the produce of different soils and seas, plants and animals, and to the regional character of different island peoples—separate, insular, fractionalized (and proud of their differences). The basic foodstuffs and condiments become more interesting when explored among insular places.

The northwest coast of Luzon is the Ilocos region, a strip of land between the mountains and the sea, where five provinces share the same language, food and tough challenges of nature. Ilocanos are frugal and hardy, relying on what can be coaxed from the dry, hot land. They eat meat sparingly, preferring vegetables and rice for the bulk of their diet.

Pinakbet (page 57) is a popular vegetable medley identified with the Ilocanos, a combination of tomatoes, eggplant and bitter melon, lima beans, okra, and squash—all bound together with bagoong, a salty sauce made from fermented fish or shrimp. Ilocano meat dishes are very delicious but tend to lean toward high cholesterol: Lomo, a pork liver and kidney soup; Longganisa (page 47), a fatty ground-pork sausage enjoyed for breakfast; and Bagnet, dried pork belly, deep fried with bagoong.

Two well-loved cuisines in the rice-and-sugar lands of Central Luzon—Pampanga and Bulacan—claim superiority over the others. In Pampanga, food is a major preoccupation; the cuisine is ornate and lavish, like their woodcarving. Many exotic dishes are attributed to land-locked Pampanga: fried catfish with buro, a fermented rice sauce; fermented crabs; frogs or milkfish in a sour soup; fried mole crickets, and Tosino, cured pork slices.

As a major sugar-producing province, Pampanga sweetens many of her dishes—especially her desserts! There are Spanish-influenced cream puffs, egg yolk custards, marzipans and meringues; plus the very native tibok-tibok (water buffalo milk blended with corn). From here also comes Bringhe (a fiesta rice made with coconut milk); Ensaymada, a buttery bun; Leche Flan (page 99), a crème brûlée made with water buffalo milk; and a great selection of sticky rice cakes.

In Bulacan, the motto is not to eat anything unless it makes you swoon with pleasure. Bulacan cooking is unhurried, old-fashioned, sure, and very varied, based on wide ingredient resources. River fish are boiled with citrus or in palm wine, then flamed. Eels are simmered in coconut cream; saltwater fish, in vinegar and ginger. Mudfish are fermented or packed in banana stalks and buried in live coals; crabs sautéed with guava; shellfish flavored in a gingery broth. Bulakeños specialize in meat dishes: A chicken "sits" in a claypot lined with salt and is slowly roasted. Typically, Bulakan cooks claim the best Relleno and Galantina (stuffed chicken rolls); Estofado (pork leg) and Asado (pot roast); and Kare-Kare (oxtail stewed in peanut sauce, page 79).

Homes around Manila Bay harbor Filipinos' favorite comfort foods, conjured from ingredients derived from around the metropolis. Fresh seafood comes in by the fishing port to the north; meats and fowl are trucked in from the south; vegetables and rice are grown on the plains of Central Luzon.

ABOVE: The spicy and delicious sausages from Lucban are a much-loved treat eaten at any time of the day.
OPPOSITE: One-pot Rice with Chicken, Pork and Shrimp in Coconut Milk (see recipe on page 44) is a simple, Luzon-style rice dish adapted from the Spanish.

Several dishes may lay claim to forming the "national" cuisine: Bistek (beef and onion rings braised in soy sauce, page 75); Lumpia (spring rolls); and the popular *adobo*—chicken and pork stewed in vinegar and soy sauce, garlic, peppercorns and bay leaf. Every province boasts of having the best *adobo*.

Manila's is soupy with soy sauce and garlic. Cavite cooks mash pork liver into the sauce. Batangas adds the orange hue of annatto seeds; Laguna likes hers yellowish and piquant with turmeric. Zamboanga's *adobo* is thick with coconut cream.

Three other items represent mainstream tastes and might be called "national" dishes. Sinigang, the lightly boiled, slightly sour soup, has a broth as tart as the heart (or taste buds) desires. An array of souring agents—unripe guavas, tamarind leaves and flowers, *kamias,* tomatoes—help make a home-cooked *sinigang* of seafood or meat and vegetables as varied as the 7,000 islands.

There is the stew known as Dinuguan—basically pig blood and innards simmered with vinegar and hot peppers. Most regions do the Dinuguan stew in their own versions.

Finally there's Lechon, the whole roast pig or piglet, star of many fiesta occasions. Lechon is slowly roasted over live coals, basted regularly—and made crisp and luscious. The tasty sauce is concocted from the pig's liver, simmered with vinegar, sugar and herbs.

From the surrounds of Laguna de Bay, the heart-shaped lake of the Southern Tagalog provinces, a rustic and honest cuisine evolved. The lake and the mountains are the sources for carp cooked in a sour soup, tilapia stuffed with tamarind leaves, and lake shrimp simmered in thick coconut cream.

Farther south, the waters of Batangas provide many fish for the table. Ocean tuna is layered and slowly cooked in an earthenware pot, freshwater sardines come from Taal Lake,

and fermented fish *bagoong* comes from Balayan town. Batangas Province is renowned, too, for its beef industry, its Bulalo (oxtail soup including the bone marrow, page 37) and her strong *barako* robusta coffee. In Quezon the preferred meat is *carabao* or water buffalo, stewed in a spicy tomato sauce. And the preferred noodle dish is Pancit Habhab—noodles scooped into a banana leaf pocket and eaten like an ice cream cone.

The Bicol region—six provinces along the southeastern peninsula of Luzon—is a lush land famous for the majestic Mayon Volcano, the smallest fish in the world, coconut forests, *pili* nuts—and spicy-hot coconut-creamy food! It has oft been said that the Bicolano farmer, in the face of frequent typhoons plaguing the region, ties down his indispensable *sili* (chili pepper) plants before looking after his wife.

Bicol is synonymous with *gata*, coconut cream. *Sili* and *gata* combine deliciously, especially in the famous Bicol dish called *pinangat*. Little bundles of *gabi* (taro) leaves are filled with shredded taro leaves and bits of tasty meat; the bundles are simmered in *gata*, and laced with a fistful of chilies.

The Visayas are the big island group in the center of the archipelago, where cuisines reflect the influence of the Chinese and the taste of the seas. Iloilo City is famous for genteel households, languid lifestyles—and delicious noodle soups. Pancit Molo (page 43) is a hearty soup of

shrimp, chicken and pork dumplings. Also, the delectable Lumpiang Ubod (page 65): heart of palm in soft crepes.

Bacolod and Iloilo share credit for *binakol*, a chicken soup based not on chicken stock but on *buko*, the sweet water of the young coconut. Bacolod also cooked up *inasal*, a barbecued chicken marinated in a heady mixture of citrus and annatto seeds.

Down Visayas way, *kinilaw* is at its pristine best. *Kinilaw* refers to the marinating of the freshest fish, shellfish or meat in vinegar or other souring ingredients—for eating raw. In Dumaguete, *kinilaw* is prepared with palm-wine vinegar, lime juice, chilies and coconut cream.

In Mindanao, the frontier land of the far south, everyday cuisine is more Malay in influence and distinctly exotic in taste. Spices are used generously: turmeric, ginger, garlic, chilies and roasted coconut. Seafoods are eaten raw, broiled or fried; or put in soups with lemongrass, ginger and green papayas; or coconut cream and turmeric. Chicken is served in curry; or combined with softened taro in a stinging soup.

Root crops are served, alongside the staple rice. Cassava is boiled and grated into cakes; rice appears as *puso*, "hearts", cooked in woven coconut fronds. Glutinous rice is often mixed with shrimp, spices, or coconut milk; or cooked with turmeric and pimento. The most exotic fruits of the country are found in Mindanao: durian, *marang*, mangosteen, and *lanzones*.

Zamboanga is a Catholic town with a distinct Spanish accent on her cuisine. *Cocido*, the traditional Sunday platter, is prepared like its Iberian prototype, with sausage, salted pork, pork ribs, sweet potatoes, corn and cooking bananas. Zamboanga has several very unique dishes—*tatos*, big ugly crabs that taste of the coconut meat they like to feed on; and *curacha*, the weirdest crab with the sweetest flavor.

Filipinos break bread together on special occasions and at every excuse. The humblest peasant shares his meal with a stranger. That sharing attitude toward food—so expressive of human bonds—ensures the survival of Philippine cuisine.

OPPOSITE TOP: Bringing in the day's catch of freshly caught tuna, General Santos City, Mindanao.
OPPOSITE BELOW: Picking strawberries outside Baguio, in the province of Benguet. Baguio, which is on average about 50°F cooler than the lowlands, is a popular summer escape for heat-weary Filipinos.
ABOVE: Bananas, gourds and tomatoes are not just for eating. Local produce is used to decorate the houses in Lucban during the fiesta of San Isidro Labrador.

Fiesta Feasting

by Doreen G. Fernandez

At four in the morning a band marches through the streets, waking the townspeople for the fiesta. Soon church bells ring, calling them to Mass to celebrate the feast of the patron saint—the Blessed Virgin in her many attributes, or saints of the religious orders that worked at Christianizing the country.

After the church rites, each town celebrates with elements of indigenous and Hispanicized custom: religious processions in which the statue of the saint is borne through town; folk theater like *komedya* and *sarswela*, all free to the public; games (e.g. water buffalo races) and fireworks; and abundant food and feasting.

In the old times, all homes were open to all comers. The town of Lucban, Quezon, dedicated to San Isidro Labrador (St Isidore the worker), proudly celebrates with food in a unique way. The houses lining the designated procession route are decorated with the varied fresh produce of the area. Rice stalks, bananas in bunches, vegetables, white gourds, squashes, green and ripe mangoes, coconuts, fish-shaped bread, succulent whole roast pigs, and especially the multi-colored rice wafers called *kiping*, decorate, even cover, the facades of houses. The owners compete not only for the

cash prize offered by the town, but for the attention of their neighbors, in the promise of another year, the good fortune of another harvest, and the joy of being together as Lucbanin.

This *Pahiyas* festival ends with the afternoon procession which, led by the saint's statue, goes rapidly through the decorated streets, as the homeowners strip their homes and throw the food gifts down to the participants. All day the homes are open to neighbors, friends from other towns, even strangers are welcomed, and the traditional *jardinera* (a meat loaf) is invariably served to all.

In Angono, Rizal, a lakeside town, the celebration is water-based. For the November feast of San Clemente, each *barangay* or neighborhood rehearses a set of marchers—women and girls in native garb (a different color per village), wearing wooden clogs and carrying miniature paddles. With several marching bands from Angono and neigh-

boring towns, they stomp through the streets in a particular rhythm, followed by men and boys carrying cans of water and laughingly trying to drench bystanders and each other—all the way to the edge of the Laguna de Bay (lake on the shore of the town of the Bay).

San Clemente and his entourage, including the parish priest and a band, are loaded onto a large boat decorated with greenery and taken for a short trip around the part of the lake bordering the town. The priest blesses the lake, the people and the fish traps. Many of the marching participants march, undeterred, right into the lake, musical instruments and all, and follow the boat as far as they can. The return trip to the church is raucous and water-drenched—participants throw water at all comers while house-owners train hoses on them. With San Clemente safely in church again, the feasting goes on. Every home serves *pancit*, *menudo*, *kare-kare*, and usually the town specialty, duck stewed and then fried crisp.

In Pakil, Laguna, the feast of our Lady of Turumba is celebrated with a procession in which only men participate, bearing her through the streets as they dance and sing.

Quiapo, in the heart of Manila, is the domain of the Black Nazarene, a statue of Christ bearing the cross. On his feast (January 9), the district is impassable, with thousands of devotees crowding the streets. Men in the hundreds vie for the honor of taking turns pulling on the ropes of the *carroza* bearing the image. Women pray and pass the men handkerchiefs to wipe against the statue (to bring them grace). Guests crowd at the windows of houses, looking down on the spectacle. And the feasting goes on.

San Dionisio, Paranaque, is known for its *komedya* during the feast of the eponymous saint. The good folk of the town believe that the discerning St. Dionisius prefers *komedya* (a full-length play in verse derived from European metrical romances, and featuring adventures in love and war) to any other kind of play, and if the saint is not pleased with the day's offering, rain will fall on the fiesta.

In Silay, Negros Occidental, a recent practice revives the *sarswela* tradition, this time written, scored, staged and presented by the different *barangays*, in a contest part of celebrating the feast of St. Didacus on November 13. The musical comedies feature the concerns, customs and aspirations of farmers, fishermen, and urban folk, Silay now being a city.

In the old, more leisurely days, fiesta preparations started weeks before the actual day. The women brought down and laundered curtains and table linen, washed and polished the silver and porcelain. The saints' statues were given fresh clothes and their jewelry (gifts of devotees) was taken out of vaults. Tenant farmers and their wives came in from the farms, bearing provisions—pigs and chickens, fruits and vegetables—and offering help. Cooks brought their best-loved knives, and soon the yards around large houses were filled with willing hands chopping, washing, cooking food in vats, butchering and roasting pigs whole, as large-eyed children watched in mounting excitement.

On the day of the fiesta, the large table in the main dining room was laid, edge to edge, with the best the host could offer: a whole *lechon*, the quintessential fiesta dish; in Batangas, whole broiled *maliputo* from the Pansipit River; in Bulacan delicate milk pastilles in handcut paper wrappers and whole fruits in syrup etched with floral designs; in Ermita, luxurious stuffed capons Spanish style; in Nueva Ecija, constellations of rice cakes; in Pampanga, fat crayfish in sour broth; everywhere, the regional noodles (*pancit*)—all the specialties of the home, town and region. The host would welcome the parish priest, the mayor, town officials, important personages and relatives. He might even go out to the street to coax the guests in. Feasting would go on throughout the day, with many seatings, and changes of menu from breakfast to lunch, *merienda* and dinner. At the end guests and workers are given packets of food to take home to the unfortunates who were not able to attend the fiesta.

At the September feast of our Lady of Peñafrancia in Naga City, guests from other towns would start coming a week before, in carriages and carabao-drawn carts bearing not only guests but servants, bedding and provisions. They would stay with relatives (no hotels then), but set up temporary households. When the feast was over, they might move on to another fiesta in another town, since these religio-social events range through the year. They not only provide evidence of the Christianization of the country, and the industry of friars who assigned saints to each city and town, but also of the communal feeling that binds Filipinos.

The fiesta is essentially an act of thanksgiving to the patron saint for intercession, to friends and neighbors for help and support through the year, and to God and nature for bounty and survival.

OPPOSITE: The festival of Ati-Atihan in the Visayan province draws crowds of visitors who come to revel in the colorful celebrations. Like many Filipino fiestas, Ati-Atihan represents a blend of both pagan and Christian beliefs. BELOW: The tantalizing sight of a fiesta table. The *lechon*, or spit-roasted pig, takes pride of place in this array of festive dishes at the Villa Escudero.

Dining and Cooking in the Philippines

A flourishing restaurant scene in a country where people eat five meals a day

by Millie Reyes

By nature Filipinos are social and gregarious, eager to share their selves—and their food—with family and friends. Whatever their tastes, eating is a way of life, an expression of being alive marked by munching, munching and more munching! Every occasion is an excuse for a tasty spread: wedding, birthday, anniversary or wake; meeting, workshop or prayer session. Any event will do to gather company and top off the affair with food!

Whether at home or in a restaurant, Filipinos love to eat communal-style, all together in an informal social gathering called a *salu-salo*. The components of a typical Filipino meal—fresh fish or other seafood; chicken, pork or beef; vegetables; hearty soups mixed with coconut and noodles—are arrayed around a large container of steamed white rice. (Meals must include the staple, rice, or else a Filipino feels like he hasn't eaten at all.) The delectable spread allows diners to feast first with their eyes (Filipinos are *takaw-mata*, greedy-eyed!). Then they partake with gusto—with fork in the left hand, spoon in the right—all the better to mix and match, and merrily combine the varied dishes with heaps of rice and accents of dipping sauces.

Eating is done frequently. On an ordinary day, there are generally five small but tasty meals to munch through—breakfast; morning *merienda* (10 am snack); lunch; afternoon *merienda* (4 pm snack), and dinner. Filipinos eat rice from morning 'til night, supported by rice cakes, nuts, and sugary snacks in-between. Plus there's happy hour and the traditional *pulutan* or finger-foods, the sometimes exotic "appetite-ticklers" that accompany the pre-dinner beer. ("Filipinos are always eating, everywhere, even in the workplace!"—says a bewildered Westerner.) Sheer madness?

There is a method to this eating madness! Like the Filipinos' grace with life itself, Philippine food comprises a spontaneous, flexible affair, based on an intuition for proportions, a native sense of balance, and a wide array of "complementary" flavors. At its simplest, Filipino ingredients undergo several basic ways of cooking—boiling, steaming, roasting, sour-stewing, or raw, *au naturel*. Native cuisine remains mostly gentle on the palate: redolent with oil and ginger as in Chinese tradition; rich with coconut, as in the Malay; or savory with garlic, onions and tomatoes, as in the Spanish. Compared to her neighbors' fiery or curried fare, Philippine cuisine is more reserved: a naive cuisine accented at table by strong-flavored condiments.

What's most unique to the Filipino eating tradition is the *sawsawan*—the mixing and matching of cooked foods with salty, sour or savory dipping sauces, called *sawsawan*. These myriad table sauces in tiny plates turn the bland white rice and the simply roasted seafood and meats into a meal that's sour, salty, sweet-salty or even bitter-sour—as one chooses. The most common condiments are: *patis* (fish sauce), *toyo* (dark soy sauce), *suka* (native vinegar), and *bagoong* (dried shrimp paste). These conspire tastily with garlic, ginger, red chili peppers, peppercorns, onions, tomatoes, *wansoy* (coriander leaves or cilantro), *kamias* (sour fruit) and kalamansi limes (small native limes).

In the good old days, hearty Filipino food was found mainly at home, cooked by homebound mothers! (Eating out to celebrate an occasion meant going together to a Chinese restaurant.) The closest thing to a Filipino food outlet was The Aristocrat by Manila Bay, founded in 1936 by the matriarch Engracia Cruz Reyes. It had started as a rolling store selling *dinuguan* (a dark stew of innards), *pancit molo* (dumpling soup), *sotanghon* (chicken broth with cellophane noodles), *pancit luglog* (a noodle dish with seafood garnish), and their special Roast Chicken Honey. Through four generations, The Aristocrat evolved into a full-blown family restaurant—an all-occasion venue with casual dining atmosphere—and a local touchstone: a place where everyone high and low gravitated to relish eating something that was truly native Filipino.

By the 1970s, family-sized Filipino restaurants proliferated around Manila, many specializing in chicken of varied styles. Customers adjusted to the fast-paced urbanization, and restaurants answered their eating-out needs. Playing on cityfolks' nostalgia for home-style cooking and provincial days, restaurants named Sulu, Zamboanga and Josephine's comprised a new breed in eateries. They focused on traditional seafood cooking (like *rellenong isda*, stuffed baked fish, or *sinigang*, a sour-broth seafood soup)—and usually served their comfort fare with folk-dancing shows! The innovative Grove marketed a daily banquet of the spicy chili and coconut milk dishes from Bicol Province. The traditionally provincial concept of *kamay an*—eating without the use of dining utensils—was successfully parlayed into a popular fad by the Kamayan Restaurant.

Today Manila's restaurant chains provide the "comfort foods" of the middle-class; their traditional cooking styles are declared in their neon-signed names: Ihaw-Ihaw (all-grilled foods); Pinausukan (smoked foods), Bakahan At Manukan (beef and chicken place); Sinangag ATBP (fried rice and more). One popular Filipino restaurant chain, Barrio Fiesta, features a festive rural atmosphere and specializes in crispy *pata* (crispy fried pork knuckles)—and sometimes singing cooks and waiters too.

OPPOSITE: Intramuros, the historic walled fortress-city by Manila Bay has become a fashionably nostalgic place to celebrate rites of passage, particularly lavish weddings.

Along with urbanization came "fast-food centers", corner-to-corner food concessionaires lining the basements of shopping malls. Filipino office workers in Makati or Malate now troop to the nearest air-conditioned fast-food center, where they find upmarket versions of the traditional *carinderia* (diner) or the proletarian *turo-turo* (point-point) stall, where a variety of home-cooked dishes are displayed at the counter and diners point out their choices, which are served along with a mound of white rice.

On the higher end of the market, amid the gentrification of Manila, there's a new spate of specialty or theme cafes and bistros, which are distinctly Filipino in form and content. Eateries don cozy bistro airs, while they present interesting Filipino fare. Some favorites around the city are Cafe Adriatico in Malate, Trellis in Quezon City, Barasoain in Makati, and Ilustrado in Intramuros. Some eateries specialize in the cuisine of a particular region of the islands; Bistro sa Remedios and Patio Mequeni, both in Malate, serve the traditional, delicious and sometimes exotic Pampanga cuisine. Gene's Bistro in Quezon City and Cafe Ysabel in San Juan serve neo-Filipino menus, with creative accents of European derivation.

Manila's top hotels have also incorporated authentic Filipino cuisine in their high-priced food outlets. The Manila Hotel has Cafe Ilang-Ilang, Holiday Inn-Pavilion has Cafe Coquilla, and Westin Philippine Plaza has Cafe Plaza, where Filipino chefs' native expertise is amply showcased, especially during regional food festivals. The Makati Shangri-La and EDSA Heritage Hotel also serve some of the finest local cuisine to elite standards. Any venue will do. When good food is abundant and shared with friends, this best exemplifies the true Filipino spirit. One can only burp with joy!

The Filipino Kitchen
The traditional Filipino kitchen is a concept fast fading in the city; the old-fashioned cooking room exists intact today only in rare provincial settings or recreated house museums. The indigenous implements of stone, clay, wood or coconut shell, once used widely in kitchens, are now in the hands of antique collectors who have preserved the *objets* for their pleasing forms. But the implements' functions have been taken over by the mass-produced tools and modern appliances of the 20th century. From that provincial kitchen—where Filipino cooks created their delectable native dishes—several traditional tools and methods are worth savoring here.

The typical Philippine kitchen was usually hidden from the public view, as it was a small, smoky, and basic affair. The rural kitchen was comprised of several simple clay stoves propped on an ashy shelf, clay pots of different sizes, cast-iron pots and pans, sundry wood and bamboo implements, and food-processing tools fashioned from heavy stone.

Kalans are bulbous clay stoves, shaped to bear a wood-fire in their bellies while they hold the pots and pans over the flames. Small sticks of wood peek through the front opening, while the cooking fire is kept going by well-placed blowing through a bamboo straw (called an *ihip*). It is a labor-intensive process: The flames are controlled by the constant removal and replacement of the glowing coals, perpetually adjusting the heat, depending on what the dish requires. Gas burners and electric stoves have, of course, replaced the wood-fires and *kalans* of old, but the new technology cannot duplicate the unique flavors that emerge from the gentle, hand-tended method.

Palayoks are the red earthenware pots used for boiling soups and steaming rice. (Traditionally, white rice is cooked with banana leaves lining the *palayok's* bottom and a fragrant pandan leaf tucked among its grains just before it's done.) *Kawalis* are the versatile woks made of cast-iron with curved-bottoms; the parabolic pans are used for just about everything else: stir-frying, deep-frying, braising, sautéing or making sauces. The *kawalis* are also used for steaming: foodstuffs are wrapped in *buri* or banana leaves and propped over boiling water. The giant metal pans called *kawas* are usually brought out for fiestas, when the communal cooking is done outdoors over open fires. Baking a native cake like the *bibingka* is done by setting hot coals over and under a clay pot lined inside with banana leaves. And drinking water was kept cool in *bangas*—large earthenware jugs. Such native kitchenware is being overtaken by teflon pans and electric rice cookers which transmit new efficiency, but bypass the old country flavors.

Some native cooking implements are still sought after today for both their functionality and aesthetic form. The *almirez* is a stone or marble mortar-and-pestle, indispensable for pounding garlic and spices and for extracting juice from shrimp heads. There are also the rustic *sandok*, a wood-handled ladle with coconut-shell scoop, and the *sianse*, a wooden spatula used for food-turning and searing meats. The *gilingan* is a heavy round millstone used for grinding rice into flour (it now serves as rustic decor). A traditional cook's most important tool is often the chopping knife and *sangkalan*, the solid wooden chopping block and heavy steel cleaver which does everything from chopping a chicken to mincing meat, from bruising a stalk of lemongrass to smashing garlic cloves.

One of the more picturesque traditional implements is the coconut grater, called a *kudkuran*. This usually takes the form of a small low bench, at one end of which protrudes an iron grater with sharp corrugated teeth. The user straddles the wooden seat and manipulates a coconut expertly, to scrape the white flesh upon the grater. Sometimes the *kudkuran* is fondly called the *kabayo* (horse).

Local implements for making native cakes and sweets trace their names to Spanish origins. There are pastry pots and molds of varying sizes, including the *lanera*, a cooking mold for the egg yolk custard called *leche flan*; the *chocolatera* or *batidor*, a brass pot for whipping and cooking chocolate; and the *tacho*, a two-handled copper pan for cooking jellies and pastillas candies. The *garapinera* is a hand-cranked machine for making ice cream.

With time and the modern American kitchen as model, Filipino households have adopted the conveniences of high technology, while retaining many of their traditional (and messy) methods of food preparation. Thus, there are generally two kitchens in the typical urban Filipino home. The so-called "dirty kitchen" (perhaps a holdover from the outdoor prep-area of the provincial fiesta) is where the kitchen helpers do the basic prepping: cleaning the seafood, dressing the chickens, pounding the shrimp, chopping the vegetables, barbecueing the meat. The "clean" kitchen is where the cook uses his or her modern appliances — blenders, mixers, microwave, rice cookers and teflon pans—before serving up delectable dishes to family and friends. The Filipino kitchen has come a long way from rustic days.

Cooking Methods

The four cooking methods that are the foundation of Filipino cookery are boiling (*nilaga*), grilling (*ihaw*), roasting and steaming (*halabos*); cooking methods that comply with the modern-day demand for healthy food and cooking. It was not until the arrival of the Spanish that sautéing (*guisado)* or frying in oil or lard came into use and that process was Filipinized and added to the basic forms of Filipino cookery.

Boiling, or *nilaga*, is the basis for many of the best-loved Filipino dishes, for example, *sinigang*, the pride of indigenous cuisine. *Sinigang* are soups or very liquid stews in which meat, fish or vegetables are combined with a souring agent. The choice of souring agent—or *pampasim*—is vast: lime, ripe guavas, starfruit, tamarind or even young tart pineapple.

The most famous of the many *nilaga* is Bulalo (page 37), which consists of boiled beef leg bone containing mar-

row with cartilage attached, plus meat and lettuce. Bulalo's flavor depends on the texture and consistency of the beef, the size and quality of the bone, and the duration of boiling time in liquid that is little else but water, salt and pepper.

The ubiquitous *adobo*, both a specific dish and a method of cooking in which pork, chicken, fish, seafood or vegetables are cooked in vinegar with garlic and pepper, depends on braising and simmering for flavor and tenderness. In the days before refrigeration became commonplace, the *adobo* served as a delicious way of preserving food.

Kinilaw is another preserving process that has produced an appetizing dish that is the Filipino version of the Spanish *ceviche*. Raw fish or shrimp are marinated or "cooked" in vinegar, salt and pepper. Visayans favor using fresh fish while the Ilocanos and Pampangos opt for *kilawing kambing*—goat steeped in vinegar and spices.

The wondrous *lechon* or roast pig, epitome of the Filipino roasting process, could have been borrowed from the Spanish delicacy *cochinillo asado*—roast suckling pig. Or, maybe it was learned from our Poly nesian neighbors who roast whole pigs on hot stones.

Steaming is another important cooking method. Most steaming is done in a wok and many dishes to be steamed are wrapped first in banana leaves which impart a subtle flavor to the food and preserve its moisture. The leaf is wiped clean and then softened in hot water before wrapping the food.

Finally, there is *ginataan*, the generic term for any dish cooked with coconut milk, of which there are many in the Philippines.

OPPOSITE TOP: A carved wooden block used to imprint a pattern on cookies. The carvings on these cookie molds are usually floral or abstract patterns, or even images of saints. OPPOSITE BELOW: The indispensible mortar and pestle. TOP: Large cooking ladles or spoons made from coconut shells are often used in the Filipino kitchen. The traditional bamboo strainer or *salaan* is both functional and elegant. BELOW: Traditional bamboo basket with a variety of uses: storing food, carrying lunch and for a trip to the market.

Authentic Filipino Ingredients

Annatto seeds (*atsuete*) are used as a natural food coloring. The dark red-dish-brown seeds are soaked in warm water or fried in oil, then pressed to extract their coloring to make Annatto Water and Annatto Oil (page 29). They color foods an orange to red tinge. The seeds have no flavor and are discarded after the color is extracted. Annatto seeds are sold in plastic packets in Asian specialty shops.

Asian eggplants (*talong*) are the long or slender, purple-skinned variety. Round Mediterranean eggplants may be used instead but these have more moisture than the Asian variety. They should be lightly salted and allowed to "sweat" for about 30 minutes to remove some of the moisture before cooking.

Bagoong is the salty, fermented shrimp or fish paste used as a flavoring in many Filipino dishes. *Bagoong* comes in 2 varieties: **fermented baby shrimp** (*bagoong alamang*) made of tiny dried shrimp, which is very much like the Malaysian *chinchalok*, and **fish paste** (*bagoong balayan*), which

is a thick, fermented paste made from *dilis* or young herring-type fish. *Bagoong* is an acquired taste, so use sparingly. Substitute Indonesian *trasi*, Malaysian *belachan* or Thai *kapi* or fish sauce.

Bamboo shoots are the crisp, mild-flavored shoots of the bamboo plant. They are available precooked—whole or sliced—in vacuum packs in well-stocked supermarkets. These pre-cooked shoots are crunchy and have a savory sweetness. They are much easier to use than fresh shoots, which must be boiled for at least an hour before use. Canned shoots are not as tasty, and when used should be drained, rinsed and boiled in hot water for 10 minutes beforehand. Store unused shoots in the refrigerator, immersed in water. If you change the water daily, bamboo shoots keep for up to 10 days.

Banana heart or banana blossom (*puso ng saging*) is the tender, inner-most portion of the young banana flower, often cooked as a vegetable. It is available fresh or dried, canned in water or brine. Canned hearts must be rinsed and blanched before use. One can of banana heart is equivalent to 2 fresh hearts. Available in Asian food stores.

Bean sprouts grown from mung beans are the common variety sold in supermarkets. Soybean sprouts, a larger variety, take slightly longer to cook than mung bean sprouts. Purchase sprouts fresh since they lose their crisp texture quite quickly. Bean sprouts will keep in the refrigerator, immersed in water, for a few days. The straggly roots and seed coats can be pinched off just before use. They are available in the produce section of supermarkets.

Bitter melon (*ampalaya*) is a small green gourd with a wrinkled skin and a distinctively bitter taste. Prior to cooking, it should be rubbed with salt and left to stand for an hour to reduce the bitterness, and then the salt is rinsed off. Perhaps because Asians believe that anything bitter is good for you, bitter melons are thought to have medicinal properties. Available from Asian grocers. Substitute bottle squash, zucchini or cucumber.

Black beans are heavily salted, fermented black soybeans. They are used sparingly to season fish and meat dishes. Sold bottled in Asian food stores, they keep for several months in the refrigerator. Black beans are often sold already mixed with garlic or chili. If using this type of mixture, reduce the amount of garlic or chili called for in the recipe.

Cassava (*kamoteng*) is a long, dark brown tuber with a rough skin and white flesh. It is often grated and used to prepare cakes and snacks. The starchy white root is steamed and eaten with sugar, or grated and mashed into tapioca paste or flour for delicacies like *suman* and *bibingka*. Frozen cassava is available in some Asian food stores. **Cassava leaves** are the tender young leaves from the top of the plant. They are boiled and eaten as a green vegetable in many parts of Asia.

Caul fat is the veil-like membrane that lines the pork abdomen. To prepare sausages or meat bundles, lay a piece of the membrane on a work table, place a filling in the center and fold the membrane over it. If the caul fat is stiff, soak it in warm water for an hour to soften before use. When frying, place the sausage seam side down to seal the caul fat. Available from butchers.

Chayote (*sayote*) is an oval, pale green squash with a small white seed. When boiled, the seed is not only edible, but very delicious. Available in well-stocked supermarkets and Latino or Filipino grocery stores. Zucchini is a good substitute.

Chicharon, or deep fried pork cracklings, are thin pieces of pork rind that are boiled, grilled and then deep-fried until crisp. Available ready-to-eat in packets in Filipino specialty stores.

Finger-length red chilies

Bird's-eye chilies

Chilies come in many varieties in Asia

but only two of them are commonly used in the Philippines; small, very hot bird's eye chilies (*siling labuyo*) and the finger-length red or green chilies (*siling mahaba*) which are also quite hot. Deseed chilies to reduce the heat. Generally, the smaller the chili, the hotter it is.

Chili leaves are the young, freshly plucked leaves from the chili plant. They are very delicate, so a little cooking suffices. Available wrapped in plastic in Filipino specialty stores. If difficult to obtain, look for a neighbor with a chili plant or grow your own. Substitute spinach.

Chinese or Napa cabbage (*pechay*) has tightly packed white stems and pale green leaves. It has a mild, delicate taste and should only be cooked for a few minutes to retain its color and crunchy texture when served. Chinese cabbage is a good source of calcium, potassium and iron, and is often eaten in soups. Available year-round in supermarkets.

Chinese celery (*kinchay*) stems are very slender and fragrant, more of a herb than a vegetable. The leaves are strongly flavored and more pungent than normal celery, and are generously used to garnish a variety of Chinese dishes. Substitute celery leaves or Italian parsley.

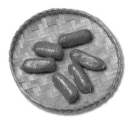

Chorizo de Bilbao are dried, Spanish-style pork sausages. They are usually sliced and added to stews. Widely available in Filipino, Hispanic and European food markets. Substitute pepperoni, garlic sausages or any spicy sausage.

Coconut is widely used in Filipino cooking. Fresh young coconut (*buko*) has a refreshing juice and sweet, soft flesh. Young coconut strips, also known as *buko* strips, are sold bottled or canned in Filipino grocery stores. You may also be able find frozen packets of whole or grated coconut flesh. Mature coconut (*niyog*) is grated and mixed with water, then squeezed to obtain **coconut milk** (*kakang gata*). Coconut milk is available canned and in packets in most supermarkets. Thick solids from the top of the can are coconut cream. If using fresh coconuts, obtain **coconut cream** by squeezing the flesh of one freshly grated coconut with $1/2$ cup (125 ml) water. **Thick coconut milk** is obtained by the same method, but by adding 1 cup (250 ml) of water to the flesh. **Thin coconut milk** is obtained by adding 2 cups (500 ml) of water to the same coconut flesh and squeezing it again. **Coconut oil** is extracted from simmering coconut milk while making Latik (page 99), a golden brown dessert topping.

Coconut gelatin (*nata de coco*) is a thick gelatin made from fermented coconut juice. Commercially available in many colors, it is a favorite ingredient in Halo Halo Supreme (page 102) and fruit salads. Sold as strings, cubes or diced in bottles, plastic packets or cans in Filipino specialty stores.

Coconut sport or *macapuno* is the soft, white jelly-like substance found in a variety of coconut fruits. Instead of water, the coconut is completely filled with a soft, white jelly that is a delicacy in the Philippines. Coconut sport is shaped into small colored balls or shaved into long strips and preserved in heavy syrup. Available bottled in Filipino stores.

Coriander leaves (cilantro) are widely used as a garnish and flavoring. Fresh coriander leaves have a strong flavor and aroma, and can be refrigerated in a plastic bag for up to a week. They are widely available. Substitute with parsley.

Eggroll wrappers (*lumpia*) are thin dough wrappers made from flour, water and salt. They are usually sold in packets of 25 or 50 squares. Circular or square wonton wrappers are very similar and may be substituted. These wrappers should always be kept frozen. When needed, individual wrappers should be peeled off and kept moist between damp kitchen towels to prevent them from drying out. Available in the refrigerator or freezer section of supermarkets.

Fish sauce (*patis*) is a pungent sauce made from boiled, salted and fermented fish. It is a clear or golden brown liquid sold in bottles, and is often used to flavor marinades, dressings and dipping sauces for a distinctly Filipino flavor. Fish sauce keeps indefinitely and is available in the

Asian section of the supermarket. Substitute Thai *nam pla* or Vietnamese *nuoc mam*.

Glutinous rice is a smaller, starchier version of short-grain rice. It is also known as sticky rice. Glutinous rice is used throughout Southeast Asia in desserts and cakes. Glutinous rice flour is also known as sweet rice flour.

Heart of palm (*ubod*) is the pith or core of the coconut palm. A mature coconut tree yields a tough heart, requiring a longer cooking time. A young coconut palm yields a very tender heart that is fully cooked in 15–20 minutes. It can be blanched and served in salads, or cooked as a vegetable filling for Fresh Spring Rolls (page 65). Available from Asian grocers.

Jicama (*singkamas*) is a crunchy and juicy white tuber that may be peeled and eaten raw, sliced and served with rock salt or dressing as a refreshing snack. Look for it in the produce section of Asian and Latin food stores.

Limes of two varieties are generally used in Filipino cuisine. The small and

more popular **kalamansi limes** are walnut-sized with a fragrant juice that adds a lively accent to many dishes. **Dayap**, the large local limes or lemons, are used in desserts like Leche Flan (page 99) and over coconut sport (see above) to lend a tart bite. Any other type of lime may generally be substituted.

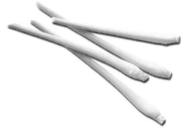

Lemongrass (*tanglad*) is a lemon-scented grass with a bulbous stem and a long, sheathed stalk. Only the lower 3 in (8 cm) of the bulb is used. It is peeled, sliced, bruised or minced, and then used to flavor sauces or stews.

Lye water or a potassium carbonate solution is added to desserts to give them the texture of commercial gelatin. Sold in supermarkets and Asian stores.

Miso is a protein-rich paste made from fermented soybeans. It has a distinctive aroma and salty flavor. Miso must be kept refrigerated. It is sold in plastic packs or tubs in the refrigerated section of food stores.

Palm nuts (*kaong*) are the fruits of the sugar palm. Sold bottled and preserved in heavy syrup. Probably too sweet for most tastes, it is a popular item in Halo Halo Supreme (page 102). Mix with ice to reduce the sweetness.

Pandanus leaves are the long, thin

leaves of the pandanus palm. They are used to infuse a delicate fragrance to steamed rice, to enhance the flavor of meats and fowl, and to impart a leafy green hue to cakes and desserts. **Pandanus extract** or syrup is sold bottled in Asian food markets. Use sparingly.

Pimentos are large, heart-shaped sweet peppers that are sweeter and more succulent than regular red bell peppers. Fresh pimentos are rare, but canned and bottled grilled pimentos are available in specialty stores.

Pinipig are toasted, crunchy young rice grains, much like patted rice cereal. They are usually eaten as a breakfast cereal or mixed into hot chocolate. They are added as an ingredient in desserts or sprinkled over sweets as a topping. Any crispy rice cereal makes a good substitute.

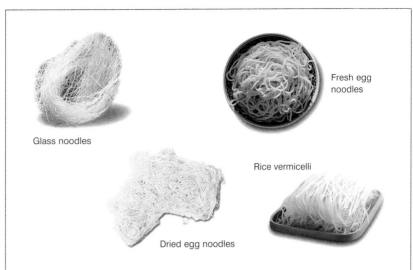

Glass noodles

Fresh egg noodles

Rice vermicelli

Dried egg noodles

Noodles in the Philippines are commonly made from rice, wheat and mung beans. *Pancit* is a generic term in Tagalog for noodle dishes. Among Filipinos, the most popular varieties are *kanton*—thick, round and yellow egg noodles, *bihon*—dried rice vermicelli and *sotanghon*—transparent mung-bean noodles, also known as glass, transparent or cellophane noodles.

Plantains are large cooking bananas. They look like over-sized bananas, but are less sweet and have a much firmer texture, making them suitable for preparation as a vegetable. Substitute unripe bananas or pumpkin.

Purple yams (*ube*) are tubers with grayish brown skin and sweet purple flesh. They are sold fresh in supermarkets or wet markets. *Ube* powder and prepared *ube halaya* (purple yam pudding, page 105) are available in packets and bottles in Asian stores. If using *ube* powder, see the instructions on the packet.

Sago pearls are the dried beads of sago starch obtained by grinding the pith of the sago palm to a paste, and then pressing it through a sieve. They are glutinous, with little flavor and are

often used in Asian desserts. Sago pearls must be thoroughly rinsed in cold water before cooking to remove of some of the starchiness. They are sold in various sizes and colors. Available in plastic packets in Asian food stores.

Salted eggs (*itlog na maalat*) have been boiled, stored in brine and painted dark red. They are the familiar festive "red eggs" served as a savory side dish during Chinese meals. Salted eggs are sold in most Chinese grocery stores, or see the note on page 61 for instructions to prepare your own.

Sesame oil is a strongly flavored oil used as a seasoning throughout Asia. It has a strong, nutty flavor and fragrance. It is generally mixed with vegetable oil when stir-frying or as a light seasoning at the end of cooking. Bottled sesame oil is available in most supermarkets.

Dried black Chinese mushrooms

Wood ear mushrooms

Button mushrooms

Mushrooms of several varieties are used in Filipino cooking. **Dried black Chinese mushrooms** have a strong, earthy flavor. Curly black **wood ear mushrooms** (*tengang daga*) go into clear noodle soups. **Button mushrooms** are the normal variety found elsewhere (champignons). Dried mushrooms require soaking in warm water to soften before use. These mushrooms are available in well-stocked supermarkets and Asian food stores.

Tofu is a highly versatile soybean product which may be steamed, deep-fried, pickled or fermented. Soft tofu is added to soups while firm tofu cubes are deep-fried. **Pressed tofu** (*tokwa*) is firm tofu that has been gently pressed to remove most of the water. Tofu is sold packed in plastic packets in cakes, blocks and cylinders in the refrigerated section of supermarkets.

Tamarind is the fruit of a tree that comes encased in brown pods with a thin shell that is easily cracked open. Inside is a tangy, fleshy pulp. It is commonly used as a souring agent for soups or as a flavoring. Tamarind pulp is sold fresh or dried (still in the pod), or dried in compressed blocks with the seeds removed. Tamarind juice is obtained by mashing 1 tablespoon of tamarind pulp in $^1/_4$ cup (60 ml) water, and straining the mixture. Available in well-stocked supermarkets and Asian grocery stores. Young **tamarind leaves** are used to season chicken soup in the Philippines.

Taro is a starchy root that must be peeled and boiled before serving. The tender, dark **taro leaves** of the plant are eaten as a vegetable.

Turmeric is a rhizome similar to ginger in appearance but with a vivid yellow interior that has a pleasant pungency absent in dried turmeric powder. The root is grated or ground and used as a spice and a food coloring in curries and rice dishes. Ground turmeric powder is widely available in the spice section of supermarkets, but try to find the fresh root as it has more flavor.

Vinegar in the Philippines (*suka*) comes in different color—hues of black, red and white. It is made from sago palm juice (*nipa*) or sugar cane (*kaong*). It has a mild, slightly sweet flavor with a fruity tang and is generally less sour than commercial white vinegar. Apple cider vinegar makes a good substitute. You may also use rice vinegar or white vinegar, but reduce the quantity by about a third.

Water chestnuts have a crunchy texture and a refreshing flavor when fresh. They are excellent in salads and are often added to stir-fried vegetables dishes. Fresh water chestnuts are troublesome to clean and peel, but well worth the effort. Chunks of fresh jicama (see above) are a good substitute, although canned water chestnuts are also widely available.

Water spinach is a highly nutritious leafy green aquatic vegetable with long, slender leaves and crunchy, hollow stems. Also known as *kangkung*, water convolvulus or morning glory. The young shoots may be eaten raw as part of a salad platter or with a dip. Full of flavor and nutrition, water spinach is often stir-fried with garlic or thrown into a *sinigang* stew.

Authentic Filipino Recipes

Portions

In Filipino homes, as in most Asian cultures, food is seldom served in individual portions, as rice and other side dishes are normally placed on the table for diners to help themselves. Small amounts of these dishes are eaten with copious amounts of fragrant fluffy boiled rice or glutinous sticky rice. It is thus difficult to estimate the exact number of portions each recipe will provide. As a general rule, however, the recipes in this book will serve 4 to 6 people as part of a meal with rice and three other dishes.

Filipino seasonings

The amounts of fish sauce (*patis*, which is salty and very pungent), *bagoong*, Filipino vinegar (*suka*), sugar and lime juice given in the following recipes are to be taken as approximate guides, not absolute measures. Bear in mind that you can always increase the amount of seasonings when tasting the food just before serving, whereas if you overdo it in the initial stages, it's too late to reduce the seasonings later.

Pickles, relishes and sauces

The relishes and sauces given on pages 25 to 29 can usually be stored in a well-sealed glass jar in a refrigerator for a week or in a freezer for 3 months. Some of the basic recipes also serve as appetizers or side dishes as part of a main meal, like Eggplant Sauce, Green Papaya Pickles and Green Mango Relish. It is not unusual to find a few bowls of dips and sauces on the dining table at any one time.

Ingredients

Many Filipino ingredients are now available in supermarkets outside the Philippines—like fish sauce (*patis*), fermented baby shrimp or fish paste (*bagoong*), coconut cream and lemongrass. Look for ingredients that are more difficult to find in Asian or Filipino specialty shops. You can also check the mail-order/online listing on page 112 for possible sources. If an ingredient is still difficult to locate, see pages 18 to 22 for possible substitutes.

Time estimates

Time estimates are for preparation and cooking, and are based on the assumption that a food processor or blender will be used.

Tips on cooking Filipino food

Most Filipino cooking begins with a fragrant stir-fry of garlic, onions and tomatoes before all the other ingredients go in. Also, bottles of *bagoong*, *patis* and vinegar (*suka*) should always be kept handy in the kitchen. Filipinos tend to include the young leafy greens from root and spice plants as vegetables—such as cassava leaves, tamarind leaves and chili leaves. Although difficult to come by, they provide a taste and texture to Filipino dishes that is quite unique. Chilies such as bird's eye chili (*siling labuyo*) may cause irritation to the eye. Ensure that you always wash and dry your hands well after handling them. When cooking with vinegar do not stir the mixture or cover the cooking pot until the vinegar has boiled. This prevents the dish from having the "raw" taste of vinegar.

Sweet and Sour Sauce
Agre Dulce

1 cup (250 ml) water
3 tablespoons tomato ketchup
3 tablespoons sugar
1/4 teaspoon salt
1/4 teaspoon hot sauce (Tabasco) (optional)
2 teaspoons cornstarch dissolved in 4 teaspoons water

1 Combine all the ingredients in a saucepan. Bring to a boil and simmer for 5 minutes or until the sauce thickens. Serve in small bowls with snacks or appetizers like eggrolls. Keeps in the refrigerator for a week.

Makes 1 cup (250 ml)
Preparation time: 5 mins
Cooking time: 5 mins

Miso Tomato Sauce
Sarsang Miso

1 teaspoon oil
1 clove garlic, minced
1 small onion, diced
2 small tomatoes, diced
1 tablespoon miso
1 teaspoon Filipino vinegar (*suka*) or apple cider vinegar
1/2 teaspoon ground black pepper

1 Heat the oil in a small skillet and stir-fry the garlic until golden brown. Add the onion and stir-fry until translucent. Add the tomatoes and cook until they soften.
2 Add the miso and mash the mixture with a fork until smooth. Add the vinegar and pepper, and bring to a boil. Remove from the heat and transfer to a sauce bowl. Serve with fried fish and stir-fried vegetables. Keeps in the refrigerator for a week.

Makes 1 cup (250 ml)
Preparation time: 15 mins
Cooking time: 15 mins

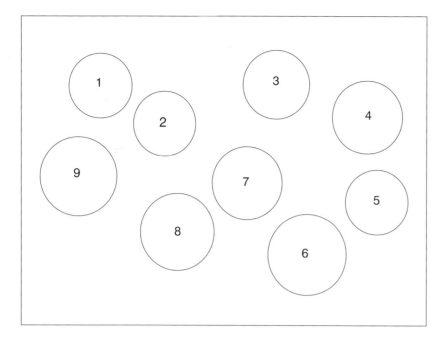

Key to photograph appearing on pages
26–27 showing a variety of authentic
Filipino relishes and dipping sauces.

1 Sweet and Sour Sauce
2 Miso Tomato Sauce
3 Liver Sauce
4 Lumpiang Sauce (page 65)
5 Eggplant Sauce
6 Green Papaya Pickles
7 Balayan Fish Sauce
8 Lime Soy Chili Dip
9 Garlic Soy Vinegar Dip

Liver Sauce
Lechon Sauce

4 oz (125 g) chicken livers or chicken
  liver pate
2 tablespoons Filipino vinegar (*suka*)
  or apple cider vinegar
$1/4$ cup breadcrumbs
3 cloves garlic, minced
1 small onion, diced
$1/4$ teaspoon salt
$1/4$ teaspoon ground pepper
1 tablespoon brown sugar
$1/2$ cup (125 ml) water

1 If using chicken livers, broil the livers until half done, about 3–4 minutes. Then extract the juices and
soft meat by pressing them through
a sieve or strainer into a bowl.
Discard the tough, stringy bits that
do not pass through the sieve.
2 Combine the strained liver meat
and juice (or liver pate) with the
other ingredients in a saucepan and
simmer for 30 minutes over medium
heat until the mixture thickens. Serve
in small bowls with Crispy Roast Pork
(page 83). Keeps in the refrigerator
for a week.

Makes 1 cup (250 ml)
Preparation time: 10 mins
Cooking time: 35 mins

Chicken Stock

1 chicken (2 lbs/1kg)
2 bay leaves
1 teaspoon peppercorns
1 cup (100 g) diced onions
1 cup (250 ml) mushroom water
  (optional)
6–8 cups ($1 1/2$–2 liters) water

1 Place all the ingredients in a pot
and bring to a boil. Reduce the heat
and simmer, covered, over low heat
until the chicken is tender, about 40
minutes. Set aside to cool.
2 Strain well and discard the solids.
Keeps in the freezer for 1–3 months.

Note: Alternatively, use canned
chicken stock, chicken stock powder or buillon cubes to prepare
instant stock (see packet instructions). If using, reduce the amount
of *patis*, salt or soy sauce called
for in the recipe as instant stocks
contain salt.

Makes 7–9 cups (2 liters)
Preparation time: 10 mins
Cooking time: 40 mins

Balayan Fish Sauce
Bagoong Balayan Guisado

1 teaspoon oil
4 cloves garlic, minced
1 small onion, diced
1 small tomato, quartered
$3/4$ cup (175 ml) fish paste (*bagoong
  balayan*)
$1/3$ teaspoon sugar
4 tablespoons Filipino vinegar (*suka*)
  or apple cider vinegar

1 Heat the oil and stir-fry the garlic
until golden brown, then add the
onion and stir-fry until translucent.
Add the tomato and cook until soft.
Add the fish paste and sugar, and
stir to dissolve.
2 Add the vinegar and simmer for
10 to 15 minutes. Remove from the
heat and serve in small dipping
bowls with Stuffed Eggplants (page
57) and other savory dishes. Keeps
in the refrigerator for a month.

Makes $1 1/2$ cups (375 ml)
Preparation time: 5 mins
Cooking time: 20 mins

Garlic Soy Vinegar Dip
Sawsawang Suka

3 cloves garlic, crushed
$1/4$ cup (60 ml) soy sauce
$1/3$ cup (90 ml) Filipino vinegar (suka) or apple cider vinegar
$1/4$ teaspoon salt
$1/4$ teaspoon ground pepper
Pinch of ground red pepper, chili powder or dried chili flakes

1 Mix all the ingredients and serve in dipping bowls with grilled meats. Keeps in the refrigerator for 6 weeks.

Makes $1/2$ cup (125 ml)
Preparation time: 5 mins

Green Mango Relish
Sawsawang Mangga

14 oz (400 g) unripe mangoes (about 1–2 mangoes), peeled, pitted and grated to yield $1^1/2$ cups of grated mango
$1/2$ small onion, diced
$1/2$ small tomato, diced
$1/2$ teaspoon fermented baby shrimp (bagoong alamang)

1 Mix all the ingredients in a bowl and set aside for 10 minutes. Serve as an appetizer or an accompaniment to rice and crispy fried fish. Keeps in the refrigerator for a week.

Makes 2 cups (500 ml)
Preparation time: 10 mins

Lime Soy Chili Dip
Toyo't Kalamansi

$1/4$ cup (60 ml) soy sauce
3 tablespoons kalamansi lime juice or regular lime juice
2 cloves garlic, minced
3 green bird's eye chilies (siling labuyo), bruised

1 Mix all the ingredients in a bowl. Serve as a side dish with fried noodles. Keeps refrigerated for a month.

Makes $1/2$ cup (125 ml)
Preparation time: 5 mins

Green Papaya Pickles
Achara

This Indian-influenced relish is a favorite in the Philippines. Served as a side dish to accompany fried and broiled fish or meat.

$1/2$ unripe papaya (about 10 oz/300 g)
$1/2$ cup (125 ml) Filipino vinegar (suka) or apple cider vinegar
$1/2$ cup (100 g) sugar
$1^1/2$ teaspoons salt
3 cloves garlic, thinly sliced
$1/2$ small carrot, cut into matchsticks
$1/2$ small green or red bell pepper, cut into matchsticks
1 in ($2^1/2$ cm) ginger, thinly sliced
1 small onion, finely diced
2 tablespoons raisins

1 Peel and grate the papaya into thin strips. Place the strips in a muslin cloth and squeeze out as much of the water from the papaya as possible. Then place the strips on a wide platter to dry in the sun.
2 Bring the vinegar, sugar and salt to a boil in a large saucepan. Add the papaya strips and simmer for 5 minutes. Add the rest of the ingredients and stir to mix. Cover the saucepan, turn off the heat and set aside to cool.
3 Transfer the cooled pickles to a sterilized jar or bottle. Keeps for a month in the refrigerator.

Makes $2^1/2$ cups (625 ml)
Preparation time: 50 mins
Cooking time: 10 mins

Annatto Water

$1/2$ cup (20 g) annatto seeds
$1/4$ cup (60 ml) water

1 Place the seeds in the water and crush them between your fingers to release the red color. Set aside for 30 minutes.
2 Strain and discard the seeds.

Makes $1/4$ cup (60 ml)
Preparation time: 5 mins

Eggplant Sauce
Sarsang Talong

14 oz (400 g) slender Asian eggplants (about 2 eggplants)
2 tablespoons Filipino vinegar (suka) or apple cider vinegar
1 clove garlic, minced
Salt and freshly ground black pepper, to taste

1 Grill the eggplants whole with the skins intact, turning them several times so that the skins are charred and the flesh is tender, about 15 minutes. Halve the eggplants and scoop out the flesh. Mash the flesh with a fork until smooth.
2 Mix the eggplant flesh with the rest of the ingredients in a bowl. Serve in small bowls as a side dish. Keeps in the refrigerator for a week.

Makes $1^1/2$ cups (375 ml)
Preparation time: 5 mins
Cooking time: 15 mins

Annatto Oil

$1/2$ cup (20 g) annatto seeds
$1/2$ cup (125 ml) oil

1 Fry the seeds in the oil for several minutes. Remove from the heat and set aside to cool.
2 When the oil is cool enough to touch, crush the seeds with the back of a spoon. Allow the crushed seeds to stand in the oil for 15 minutes.
3 Strain and discard the seeds.

Note: You can buy packaged annatto powder that can be added to recipes instead of Annatto Oil as a food coloring agent, or achiotina which is a prepared annatto oil sold in small bottles. Annatto Oil and Annatto Water color food an attractive hue of orange or red.

Makes $1/2$ cup (125 ml)
Preparation time: 15 mins
Cooking time: 3 mins

Fish Ceviche   Kinilaw Na Tanguigue

This excellent appetizer is similar to Spanish *ceviche*—raw fish and shellfish "cooked" in vinegar and lime juice, and seasoned with spices. The kalamansi lime juice, garlic, tomatoes and ginger give this dish a wonderfully fresh flavor.

1 lb (500 g) mackerel, sea bass, grouper or salmon fillets
$1/_2$ cup (125 ml) Filipino vinegar (*suka*) or apple cider vinegar
3 tablespoons kalamansi lime juice or lemon juice
2 cloves garlic, minced
$1/_2$ medium onion, minced
2 small tomatoes, diced
1 in ($2^1/_2$ cm) fresh young ginger, minced
1 bell pepper, deseeded, halved and cut into thin strips
$1/_2$ teaspoon salt
$1/_2$ teaspoon freshly ground black pepper
Onion, thinly sliced, to garnish

1 Clean the fish fillets and cut them into strips. Marinate the fish in the vinegar for an hour, then drain and discard the marinade.
2 Add the kalamansi lime or lemon juice and all the other ingredients to the fish. Toss lightly to mix and coat well.
3 Transfer to a bowl and chill in the refrigerator until ready to eat. Garnish with onion slices and serve.

Serves 4–6   Preparation time: 30 mins

Shrimp and Tofu Fritters   Ukoy

This crunchy appetizer is great as an afternoon snack between meals (*merienda*), or as a cocktail snack in the evening with drinks (*pulutan*).

12 fresh medium shrimp (about 8 oz/ 250 g), heads and legs discarded, shells left on
2 cups (5 oz/150 g) bean sprouts, rinsed, shells and tails discarded
$1/_2$ small cake ($3^1/_2$ oz/100 g) pressed tofu, drained and diced
4 oz (125 g) ground chicken
2 tablespoons fermented baby shrimp (*bagoong alamang*)
Oil for deep-frying
1 portion Garlic Soy Vinegar Dip (page 29), to serve

Batter
2 eggs, beaten
1 teaspoon baking powder
$1/_4$ cup (30 g) cornstarch
$3/_4$ cup (100 g) plain flour
1 tablespoon Annatto Water (page 29) (optional)
$1/_2$ cup (125 ml) water
$1/_2$ teaspoon freshly ground black pepper

1 Prepare the Garlic Soy Vinegar Dip and Annatto Water, if using, by following the instructions on page 29.
2 Make the Batter by whisking the eggs, baking powder, cornstarch, flour, Annatto Water and water together in a bowl to form a smooth, thin batter. Season with the black pepper.
3 Heat the oil in a wok or saucepan. Add the shrimp, bean sprouts, tofu, chicken and fermented shrimp to the Batter and mix well. Ladle about 3 tablespoons of the mixture into the hot oil, ensuring that each portion contains 1 shrimp and bits of all the other ingredients. Fry for 3 minutes until the fritters are golden brown, then remove with a slotted spoon and drain on paper towels. Repeat until all the mixture is used up. Serve the fritters with small bowls of Garlic Soy Vinegar Dip on the side.

Makes 12 fritters   Preparation time: 20 mins   Cooking time: 15 mins

Pork Cracklings   Chicharon Baboy

A favorite *pulutan* (finger food to accompany beer or cocktails), especially when freshly cooked and dipped in a refreshing vinegar sauce. Also available ready-to-eat in packets in Filipino stores.

2 lbs (1 kg) pork rind, cut into 1-in (2¹/₂-cm) squares
3 cups (750 ml) water
1 tablespoon salt
Oil for deep-frying
1 portion Garlic Soy Vinegar Dip (page 29)

1 Prepare the Garlic Soy Vinegar Dip by following the instructions on page 29.
2 Preheat the oven to 300°F (150°C). Boil the pork rind squares in the water and salt for 30 minutes, then drain in a colander.
3 Arrange a layer of the boiled rind on a baking pan and bake on the middle section of the oven for 3 hours. Remove the baked rinds from the oven and set aside to cool.
4 Heat the oil in a wok until very hot. Deep-fry the baked rinds over high heat until they puff up, then remove from the oil with a slotted spoon and drain on paper towels. Serve with a bowl of Garlic Soy Vinegar Dip on the side.

Serves 6–8   Preparation time: 25 mins   Cooking time: 3 hours 20 mins

Shanghai-style Eggrolls   Lumpiang Shanghai

A popular Filipinized adaptation of the Chinese eggroll, usually stuffed with meat, shrimp, carrots and crunchy water chestnuts.

8 oz (250 g) ground pork
8 oz (250 g) fresh shrimp, peeled and minced
3/4 cup (6 oz/175 g) water chestnuts or jicama (*singkamas*), peeled and diced
1 medium carrot, peeled and cut into short strips
3 cloves garlic, minced
1 spring onion, thinly sliced
1 teaspoon soy sauce
1/2 teaspoon salt
1 teaspoon freshly ground black pepper
15 eggroll wrappers (see note)
Oil for deep-frying
1 portion Sweet and Sour Sauce (page 25)

1 Prepare the Sweet and Sour Sauce by following the instructions on page 25.
2 Mix the pork, shrimp, water chestnuts, carrot, garlic, spring onion and soy sauce in a bowl. Season with the salt and pepper.
3 Place 1 heaped tablespoon of the pork-shrimp mixture on each eggroll wrapper. Roll the wrapper up tightly and seal the ends with a few drops of water. Repeat until all the filling is used up.
4 Heat the oil in a wok. Deep-fry the prepared eggrolls in the hot oil until light golden brown. Remove with a slotted spoon and drain on paper towels. Serve with a bowl of Sweet and Sour Sauce on the side.

Note: Eggroll wrappers are sold in various sizes. This recipe calls for 5 in (12¹/₂ cm) square wrappers. They are sold in packets of 25 or 50 wrappers in the refrigerator or freezer section of supermarkets. If using larger wrappers, double the amount of filling used in each eggroll.

Makes 15 eggrolls   Preparation time: 20 mins   Cooking time: 25 mins

Chicken Rice Soup with Ginger
Arroz Caldo Con Pollo

A favorite one-pot meal, this "comfort food" is especially good during the rainy season.

4 tablespoons oil
4 tablespoons minced garlic
1 large onion, diced
2 in (5 cm) fresh ginger, cut into thin slices
$^3/_4$ cup (150 g) uncooked rice, washed and drained
7 cups (1$^3/_4$ liters) water
1 lb (500 g) boneless chicken, cut into bite-sized pieces
1$^1/_2$ teaspoons fish sauce (*patis*)
  or 1 teaspoon salt with a dash of soy sauce
Freshly ground black or white pepper, to taste
Spring onion, thinly sliced, to garnish
Pinch of saffron, to garnish
Kalamansi limes or regular limes, halved, to serve

1 Heat 2 tablespoons of the oil in a pot and stir-fry half of the garlic until golden brown. Add the onion and ginger and stir-fry until the onion is translucent.
2 Add the rice and stir-fry for 5 minutes until lightly browned. Add the water and cover the pot. Increase the heat and bring the mixture to a boil, stirring occasionally. Then reduce the heat, add the chicken and simmer for another 30 minutes or until the rice and chicken are cooked.
3 While the rice is cooking, heat the remaining oil in a skillet and stir-fry the rest of the garlic until crisp and golden brown. Drain on paper towels and set aside.
4 When the rice and chicken are cooked, add the fish sauce or salt, stir and continue to simmer over low heat for another 2 minutes. Serve in individual soup bowls seasoned with black or white pepper. Garnish with the spring onion, fried garlic and saffron, and serve with lime halves on the side.

Note: This soup tastes even better when prepared a day in advance and kept overnight in the refrigerator, then reheated.

Serves 4   Preparation time: 20 mins   Cooking time: 45 mins

Beef and Banana Heart Soup Bulalo

A clear and richly-flavored soup made from beef brisket or shank and bone marrow—a hearty dish that should be eaten hot with fluffy fragrant rice.

1¹/₂ lbs (750 g) beef brisket or beef
  shank with bone marrow, cut into
  3 in (8 cm) cubes
2 large onions, sliced
2 leeks, sliced
1 fresh banana heart (about 8 oz/
  250 g, see note), sliced,
  or 8 oz (250 g) small cabbage,
  sliced
2 teaspoons fish sauce (patis)
  or ¹/₂ teaspoon salt
¹/₄ teaspoon freshly ground black
  pepper
1 cake (8 oz/250 g) pressed tofu, cut
  into bite-sized cubes

1 Cover the beef brisket or shank in water in a pot and bring to a boil for 10 minutes. Remove the beef, discard the water and clean the pot.
2 Return the shank to the pot, cover with 8 cups (2 liters) of water and bring to a boil over high heat. Boil, uncovered, until the broth has reduced by half, about 1 hour.
3 Add the onions, leeks and banana heart or cabbage, and cook for 30 minutes over medium heat. Season with the fish sauce and pepper, then add the tofu and stir to mix well. Serve hot.

Note: The beef shank is boiled twice to reduce the fat content in the soup. To prepare the banana heart, remove the tough outer layers until you reach the tender inner heart of the banana flower. Cut these tender parts length-wise into matchsticks and soak in lightly salted water to prevent discoloration until ready to use.

Serves 4–6   Preparation time: 20 mins   Cooking time: 1 hour 40 mins

Chicken Soup with Green Papaya and Ginger Tinolang Manok

This soothing and delicious chicken and ginger soup was popularized in the novel *Noli Me Tangere* by Jose P. Rizal, the Philippines' founding father and national hero.

2 tablespoons oil
5 cloves garlic, minced
1 small onion, diced
1 in (2¹/₂ cm) ginger, bruised
1 chicken (2 lbs/1 kg), cut into
  serving pieces
2 teaspoons fish sauce (patis)
  or 1 teaspoon salt
Freshly ground black pepper, to taste
5 cups (1¹/₄ liters) water
8 oz (250 g) unripe papaya, chayote
  or zucchini, peeled and cubed
2 cups (about 100 g) fresh spinach
  leaves, watercress or chili leaves,
  washed and trimmed

1 Heat the oil in a pot and stir-fry the garlic until golden brown. Add the onion and ginger, and stir-fry until the onion is translucent.
2 Add the chicken pieces and stir-fry over medium heat until partially cooked, about 3 minutes. Then season with the fish sauce and pepper. Add the water and simmer, covered, over medium heat until the chicken is tender, about 30 minutes.
3 Add the papaya, chayote or zucchini and cook until tender, about 10 minutes. Turn off the heat and add the spinach or watercress. Mix well until the vegetables are wilted. Serve immediately with rice.

Serves 4   Preparation time: 20 mins   Cooking time: 45 mins

Chicken Soup with Coconut Binakol

A favorite of former US President Bill Clinton when he came to Manila, this dish originates from the southern provinces of the Philippines where coconut production is done on a large scale.

3 tablespoons oil
6 cloves garlic, peeled and crushed
1 medium onion, diced
1 in (2$^1/_2$ cm) ginger, sliced
3 stalks lemongrass, thick lower part only, outer layers removed, inner part bruised
1 teaspoon salt
$^1/_4$ teaspoon ground black pepper
8 oz (250 g) boneless chicken, cut into bite-sized cubes
4 cups (1 liter) Chicken Stock (page 28) or 2 teaspoons chicken stock granules mixed with 4 cups (1 liter) hot water
1 young coconut, meat scraped out and sliced into bite-sized pieces, juice reserved
Salt and pepper, to taste
Coriander leaves (cilantro), coarsely chopped, to garnish

1 Heat the oil in a saucepan and stir-fry the garlic until golden brown. Add the onion and ginger, and stir-fry until the onion is translucent. Add the lemongrass, salt and pepper, and stir-fry for another 5 minutes.
2 Add the chicken and stir-fry until lightly browned. Then add the stock and bring to a boil. Reduce the heat and simmer for 45 minutes until the chicken is tender.
3 Add the coconut meat and reserved coconut juice, and simmer for another 5 minutes. Season with salt and pepper if required. Serve hot, garnished with fresh coriander leaves.

Serves 4–6   Preparation time: 25 mins   Cooking time: 1 hour

Ground Beef Stew   Picadillo

A popular Spanish-influenced dish that is so quick and easy to prepare. It may be served as a soup or stew depending on the amount of liquid added. Absolutely delicious with rice!

1$^1/_2$ tablespoons oil
5 cloves garlic, minced
10 shallots or 1 onion, diced
4 small tomatoes, diced
12 oz (350 g) ground beef
1 tablespoon fish sauce (*patis*)
  or 1 teaspoon salt
$^1/_2$ teaspoon freshly ground black
  pepper
2 potatoes, peeled and cubed
4 cups (1 liter) water
Parsley or coriander leaves (cilantro),
  coarsely chopped, to garnish

1 Heat the oil in a saucepan and stir-fry the garlic until golden brown. Add the shallots or onion and stir-fry for 2 minutes. Then add the tomatoes and cook until they soften.
2 Add the ground beef and season with the fish sauce and pepper. Stir-fry for 5 minutes to brown the meat. Add the potatoes and water, and bring to a boil. Reduce the heat and simmer, uncovered, over low heat until the beef and potatoes are cooked, about 20 minutes (add more water if needed or if you prefer a more soupy dish).
3 Ladle the stew into a large serving bowl and garnish with fresh parsley or coriander leaves. Serve hot with white rice.

Serves 4   Preparation time: 25 mins   Cooking time: 30 mins

Corn and Clam Chowder Suam Na Tulya

A favorite dish from the town of Sulipan in Pampanga Province. At the turn of the century, Sulipan, or Apalit as it was then known, was famous for its *haute cuisine*. This delicious version is from Gene Gonzalez of Cafe Ysabel in Manila.

1 lb (500 g) fresh unshucked clams, scrubbed and rinsed
4 tablespoons olive oil
1 clove garlic, minced
1 medium onion, sliced
1 in ($2^1/_2$ cm) fresh ginger, bruised
$1^1/_2$ cups corn kernels (frozen or cut from 2 fresh corn cobs)
1 cup (250 ml) clam stock
  or $^1/_2$ teaspoon seafood stock granules mixed with 1 cup (250 ml) hot water
$2^1/_2$ cups (625 ml) water
1 teaspoon fish sauce (*patis*)
  or $^1/_2$ teaspoon salt or more to taste
$^1/_4$ teaspoon freshly ground black pepper or to taste
$^1/_2$ cup (about 25 g) chili leaves, bell pepper leaves
  or $1^1/_2$ cups ($2^1/_2$ oz/75 g) spinach, washed and trimmed

1 Soak the clams in lightly salted water for 15 minutes. Drain and set aside.
2 Heat the oil in a large pot or wok and stir-fry the garlic until golden brown. Add the onion and ginger, and stir-fry until the onion is translucent. Add the clams and stir-fry over high heat for 1 minute, until the shells open. Remove the clams and set aside. Discard any clams that do not open.
3 Add the corn kernels, clam stock and water to the pot. Mix well and simmer over medium heat for 20 minutes. Season with the fish sauce and pepper. Increase the heat and return the clams to the pot. Stir to mix and cook for another 3 minutes.
4 Add the chili leaves and stir until wilted, about 3 minutes. Season with freshly ground black pepper if desired, and serve.

Note: Young chili leaves should be plucked from the top of the chili plant. This unusual and delicate vegetable has a fragrant chili-like aroma when cooked. If unavailable, substitute with bell pepper leaves or spinach.

Serves 4   Preparation time: 30 mins   Cooking time: 30 mins

Hearty Wonton Soup Pancit Molo

5 fresh medium shrimp (about 4 oz/125 g), shelled and deveined (optional)
2 tablespoons oil
5 cloves garlic, minced
1 medium onion, halved and sliced
8 cups (2 liters) Chicken Stock (page 28)
  or 4 teaspoons chicken stock granules mixed with 8 cups (2 liters) hot water
1 tablespoon fish sauce (*patis*)
  or 1 teaspoon salt
1 teaspoon freshly ground black pepper
1 spring onion, thinly sliced, to garnish

Filling
6 oz (175 g) ground pork
2 oz (60 g) fresh shrimp, shelled and minced
4 cloves garlic, minced
$1/2$ medium onion, minced
2 spring onions, minced
$1/2$ cup (100 g) water chestnuts (about 4 water chestnuts), diced
2 egg yolks
1 teaspoon salt
$1/4$ teaspoon freshly ground black pepper

Wonton Wrappers
$1^3/4$ cups (270 g) plain flour
$1/2$ cup (125 ml) water
1 egg

1 Make the Filling by combining all the ingredients in a large bowl. Set aside.
2 Make the wrappers by kneading the flour, water and egg for 10 minutes to form a smooth dough. Set the dough aside to rest for 15 minutes. Pinch about 1 tablespoon of the dough and roll it into a small ball. Place the dough ball on a floured work surface and flatten it with your palm. Roll the dough out into a $3^1/2$ in (9 cm) circle and set aside on a dry plate. Repeat with the rest of the dough to make at least 25 circular wrappers in all.
3 Scoop 1 teaspoon of the Filling onto the center of each wrapper and dab a little water on the wrapper around the Filling. Fold the wrapper around the Filling like a pouch and press to seal the edges. Set aside on a large plate. Repeat until all the Filling is used up to make 25 wonton pouches.
4 Heat the oil in a pot and stir-fry the garlic until golden brown. Add the onion and stir-fry until the onion is translucent. Add the stock, season with the fish sauce and pepper, and bring to a boil. Drop the wontons and shrimp into the stock, and cook for 5 minutes or until the wontons float to the top. Garnish with the freshly sliced spring onion and serve immediately.

Note: If you don't have time to make your own, fresh or frozen wonton wrappers are sold in plastic packets in the refrigerator or freezer sections of most supermarkets. Also available in Asian food stores.

Serves 5   Preparation time: 35 mins   Cooking time: 55 mins

Cuban-style Rice with Meat Sauce and Plantains   Arroz a la Cubaña

A hearty rice dish with a strong Caribbean influence—featuring ground meat and vegetables in a delicious sauce served with fried plantains and eggs.

3 tablespoons oil
2 cloves garlic, minced
4 shallots, diced
1 small tomato, diced
8 oz (250 g) ground beef
8 oz (250 g) ground pork
2 tablespoons soy sauce
1/2 tablespoon Worcestershire sauce
1/4 cup (50 g) raisins
1/2 teaspoon salt
1/4 teaspoon freshly ground black pepper
1/2 cup (60 g) fresh or frozen peas
3 tablespoons olive oil or peanut oil
5 oz (150 g) small plantains or unripe bananas, peeled and sliced length-wise
4 eggs
4 cups (800 g) freshly cooked rice, kept warm

1 Heat the oil in a saucepan and stir-fry the garlic until golden brown. Add the shallots and stir-fry until translucent. Add the tomato and cook until it softens. Add the beef, pork, soy and Worcestershire sauces, and cook over medium heat for 15 minutes or until the meat is browned.
2 Add the raisins, salt and pepper, and stir constantly. Add the peas and braise for a further 5 minutes. Remove from the heat and set aside.
3 In a skillet, heat the olive oil and fry the plantain slices until they are soft and caramelized on both sides, about 5–7 minutes, and set aside. Then fry the eggs in the skillet sunny-side up.
4 Arrange the cooked rice, meat, fried plantains and eggs on a large serving platter. Serve hot.

Serves 4–6   Preparation time: 15 mins   Cooking time: 20 mins

One-pot Rice with Chicken, Pork and Shrimp in Coconut Milk
Bringhe

Fresh coconut milk and glutinous rice are the main ingredients of this "poor man's" version of paella (see photo on page 9).

3 tablespoons oil
4 cloves garlic, minced
1/2 medium onion, diced
1 chicken (2 lbs/1 kg), boiled and cut into serving pieces
8 oz (250 g) pork, boiled for 15 minutes, then cubed
2 cups (400 g) uncooked rice, washed and drained (glutinous rice preferred)
1 bay leaf
1 teaspoon salt
3 cups (750 ml) thin coconut milk
1 cup (125 g) fresh or frozen peas
1 teaspoon ground turmeric
4 oz (125 g) fresh medium shrimp, shelled and deveined
3 hard-boiled eggs, halved
1 small bell pepper, deseeded and thinly sliced

1 Heat the oil in a pot or large saucepan and stir-fry the garlic until golden brown, then stir-fry the onion until translucent. Add the chicken and pork and stir-fry until browned, about 5 minutes.
2 Add the rice, bay leaf, salt, coconut milk, peas and ground turmeric, and stir the mixture to prevent it from sticking to the bottom of the pot. Reduce the heat, cover, and simmer over low heat for 20 minutes or until the meat and rice are almost cooked. Add the shrimp and simmer for another 5 minutes until they turn pink. Remove from the heat and serve garnished with the hard-boiled eggs and bell pepper.

Serves 4–6   Preparation time: 25 mins   Cooking time: 35 mins

Philippine Fried Rice   Sinangag

Rice is the staple for Filipinos and so, no meal is complete without it. Here, freshly cooked rice is served with sausages and fried fish to create a classic Filipino breakfast. The sausages and dried fish are also sold in Asian specialty stores.

4 tablespoons oil
4 cloves garlic, minced
4 shallots, diced
4 cups (about 800 g) cold cooked
  rice (refrigerated leftover rice) lightly
  flaked with $1/2$ cup (125 ml) water
1 tablespoon soy sauce
1 teaspoon salt
$1/4$ teaspoon freshly ground black
  pepper

1 Heat the oil in a wok or large frying pan and stir-fry the garlic until golden brown. Add the shallots, rice, soy sauce, salt and pepper, and stir-fry for 10 minutes, turning the rice frequently to ensure even cooking and to prevent the rice from sticking to the pan. Serve hot with the Philippine Pork Sausages and Crispy Fried Fish (see recipes below).

Serves 4   Preparation time: 10 mins   Cooking time: 15 mins

Philippine Pork Sausages   Longganisa

1 lb (500 g) ground pork
4 tablespoons Filipino vinegar (*suka*)
  or apple cider vinegar
4 cloves garlic, minced
1 teaspoon freshly ground black
  pepper
7 oz (200 g) caul fat
$1/2$ teaspoon salt

1 Mix the pork, vinegar, garlic and pepper in a large bowl. Shape the mixture into cylindrical rolls that are about 1 in ($2^1/2$ cm) thick and 3 in (8 cm) long. Place each roll on a section of the caul fat and fold the veil-like membrane over to enclose it. Form sausages in this way with all the meat and caul fat. Season the uncooked sausages with a light sprinkling of the salt.
2 Place the sausages with the overlapping folds of caul fat facing down on a lightly greased skillet and cook to seal them. Cook the sausages for 7–10 minutes, drain on paper towels and serve hot or at room temperature.

Note: You can purchase caul fat from your butcher, although you may have to reserve it the day before.

Serves 4–6   Preparation time: 25 mins   Cooking time: 15 mins

Crispy Fried Fish

8 oz (250 g) dried *biya*, goby
  or other freshwater fish
2 tablespoons oil

1 Heat the oil in a wok and fry the fish for 1 minute on either side or until light golden brown and crispy. Remove from the oil with a slotted spoon and drain on paper towels.

Note: Dried *biya* fish is available from Asian specialty stores. It is also delicious deep-fried and eaten on its own with a refreshing vinegar dip or served as a topping on stir-fried vegetables.

Serves 6–8   Preparation time: 5 mins   Cooking time: 5 mins

Paella

A Filipino adaptation of the famous Valencian dish that makes a satisfying one-pot meal for 4–6 people. Your guests will not believe how simple it is to prepare!

10 fresh medium shrimp (about 7 oz/200 g), shelled and deveined, tails intact
Salt and pepper, to taste
2 fresh crabs (about 3 lbs/1$^1/_2$ kg total)
5 cups (1$^1/_4$ liters) water
2 medium squid (about 10 oz/300 g), cleaned and cut into rings
$^1/_2$ cup (125 ml) olive oil
8 oz (250 g) pork tenderloin, cut into bite-sized pieces
$^1/_2$ teaspoon paprika or ground red pepper
2 tablespoons minced garlic
$^1/_2$ medium onion, diced
One 3-in (8-cm) *chorizo de Bilbao* or pepperoni sausage, thinly sliced
2 cups (400 g) uncooked long-grain rice
4 tablespoons canned tomato purée
1 bay leaf
1 bell pepper, deseeded and cut into chunks
Generous pinch of saffron mixed with 1 teaspoon water
$^1/_2$ cup (60 g) fresh or frozen green peas
2 hard-boiled eggs, quartered or sliced

1 Season the shrimp lightly with the salt and pepper, and set aside.
2 Boil the crabs in the water for 20 minutes or until cooked. When cooked, remove the crabs, quarter them, crack the shells and claws, and set aside. Reserve the water.
3 Blanch the squid in the reserved crab water until cooked, about 3 minutes. Remove the squid and set aside in a bowl of cold water. Strain and reserve 3$^3/_4$ cups (925 ml) of the crab-squid broth.
4 Preheat the oven to 350°F (180°C). Heat the olive oil in a large skillet or casserole dish. Add the pork, paprika, garlic, onion and *chorizo* slices, and stir-fry for a few minutes. Then add the rice and stir-fry until lightly browned. Add the tomato purée, reserved broth and bay leaf, and stir for a few minutes. Add the bell pepper and saffron, and bring to a boil.
5 Remove from the heat and bake in the preheated oven, uncovered, for 30 minutes. Arrange the seasoned shrimp, crab, squid and peas on the rice, and bake for another 5 minutes. Remove from the oven and decorate with the hard-boiled eggs. Transfer to the dining table and serve immediately.

Serves 4–6   Preparation time: 30 mins   Cooking time: 1 hour 10 mins

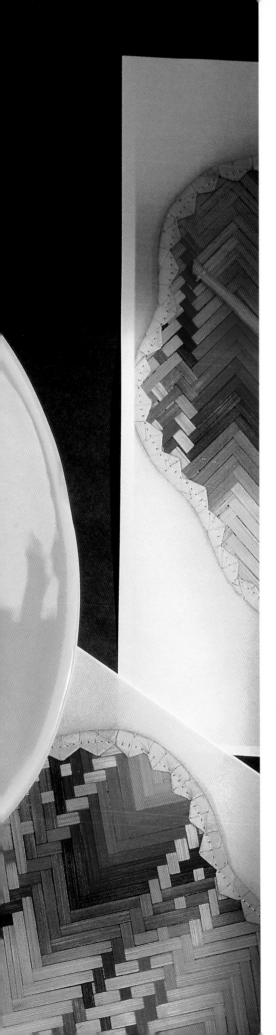

Canton-style Braised Noodles Pancit Canton

A favorite noodle dish to which meat and vegetables are added. Named after the city of Canton, but chances are, you won't find this dish there.

8 oz (250 g) fresh medium shrimp, peeled and deveined
1 egg white
1 tablespoon cornstarch
1 boneless chicken breast, sliced into thin strips
3 tablespoons oil
5 cloves garlic, peeled and crushed
1 small onion, diced
1 tablespoon black wood ear mushrooms, soaked in warm water for 20 minutes
   to soften, then sliced into thin strips
1 tablespoon fish sauce (*patis*) or soy sauce
Freshly ground black pepper, to taste
2 chicken livers, boiled and sliced
$1^1/_2$ cups (375 ml) Chicken Stock (page 28) or $^3/_4$ teaspoon chicken stock granules mixed with $1^1/_2$ cups (375 ml) hot water
1 small carrot, peeled and thinly sliced
1 stick of celery, thinly sliced
8 oz (250 g) dried Chinese egg noodles
1 tablespoon cornstarch dissolved in 2 tablespoons water
Kalamansi limes or regular limes, halved to serve

1 In a small bowl, mix the shrimp with the egg white and $^1/_2$ tablespoon of the cornstarch. In another bowl, dredge the chicken strips in the remaining cornstarch.
2 Heat the oil in a wok or saucepan and stir-fry the garlic until golden brown, then stir-fry the onion until translucent. Add the chicken and mushrooms, and stir-fry for a few minutes. Season with the fish sauce and pepper. Add the shrimp and chicken livers, and stir-fry briskly for 2 minutes.
3 Add the stock, increase the heat and bring to a boil. Add the carrot, cel-ery and dried noodles, and cook until the vegetables are done and the noo-dles are al dente, about 4 minutes. Then thicken the sauce with the corn-starch. Serve on a platter surrounded with lime halves.

Serves 4   Preparation time: 25 mins   Cooking time: 10 mins

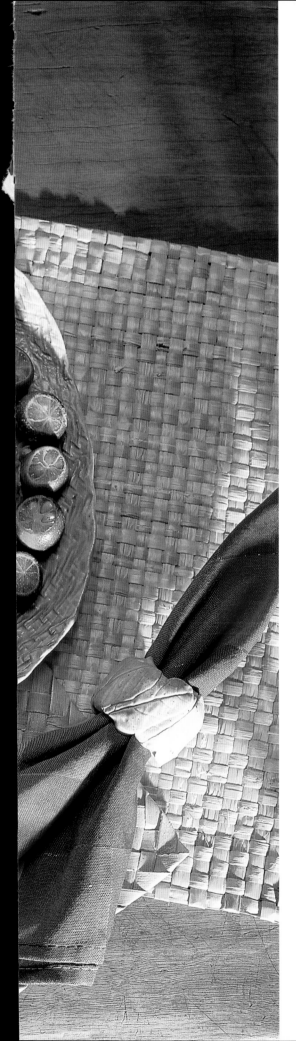

Chicken Vermicelli Sotanghon

Noodles signify long life and Filipinos consume an abundance of them. This is a popular Chinese-influenced dish in which cellophane (glass) noodles made from mung beans are the main ingredient.

4 tablespoons oil
8 cloves garlic, minced
1 large onion, diced
1 chicken breast, boiled and sliced into strips
10 dried black Chinese mushrooms, soaked in warm water to soften, drained and thinly sliced
3 cups (750 ml) Chicken Stock (page 28) or $1^1/_2$ teaspoons chicken stock granules mixed with 3 cups (750 ml) hot water
$^1/_2$ cup (125 ml) Annatto Water (page 29) (optional)
$^1/_2$ small carrot, cut into matchsticks
$^1/_2$ leek, cut into matchsticks
1 bunch Chinese celery leaves or Italian parsley, thinly sliced
6 oz (175 g) dried cellophane (glass) noodles (*sotanghon*), soaked in water for 10 minutes to soften and then cut into 6-in (15-cm) lengths
$1^1/_2$ tablespoons fish sauce (*patis*) or 1 teaspoon salt
Freshly ground black pepper, to taste
Spring onion, thinly sliced, to garnish
Kalamansi limes or regular limes, halved, to serve

1 Heat the oil in a wok and stir-fry the garlic until golden brown, then stir-fry the onion until translucent. Add the chicken and mushrooms, and stir-fry for another 2 minutes. Add the stock and Annatto Water, if using, and bring to a boil. Add the carrot, leek and celery leaves, and cook for 3 minutes.
2 Add the dried noodles and cook for 3 minutes. Season with the fish sauce and pepper, and stir to mix well.
3 Remove from the heat and transfer the food to a serving platter. Garnish with freshly sliced spring onion and serve hot with limes on the side.

Note: If using Annatto Water in the dish, reduce the amount of stock called for in the recipe by $^1/_2$ cup (125 ml).

Serves 4–6   Preparation time: 36 mins   Cooking time: 15 mins

Vegetable Stew with Tofu   Bulanglang

This flexible, affordable and easy to prepare dish is popular in rural areas and enjoyed by both landlord and tenants at mealtime.

$^1/_2$ medium onion, diced
1 medium tomato, diced
1$^1/_2$ teaspoons fish paste (*bagoong balayan*)
1 cup (100 g) butternut squash or pumpkin, cubed
$^1/_2$ cup (50 g) fresh or frozen fava beans
1 cup (250 ml) water
$^1/_2$ cake (4 oz/125 g) pressed tofu, sliced and fried
$^1/_2$ small zucchini (125 g), sliced
5 cups (8 oz/250 g) spinach or water spinach, washed and drained (optional)
$^1/_2$ teaspoon salt

1 Place the onion, tomato, fish paste, squash and fava beans in a deep saucepan. Add the water, stir and bring to a boil.
2 Add the tofu and zucchini slices, and simmer until the squash and zucchini are tender, about 10 minutes.
3 Add the spinach, if using, and cook for another 3 minutes, or until the leaves are wilted. Season with the salt and serve.

Serves 4   Preparation time: 25 mins   Cooking time: 20 mins

Stir-fried Mung Beans   Guinisang Monggo

1 cup (200 g) dried green mung beans
4 cups (1 liter) water
1 teaspoon salt
2 tablespoons oil
8 oz (250 g) pork meat, diced
6 cloves garlic, minced
1 large onion, finely diced
2 plum tomatoes, diced
3 cups (750 ml) Chicken Stock (page 28) or 1$^1/_2$ teaspoons chicken stock granules mixed with 3 cups (750 ml) hot water
1 tablespoon fermented baby shrimp (*bagoong alamang*)
1 cup (50 g) bitter melon leaves or 1$^1/_2$ cups (2$^1/_2$ oz/75 g) spinach, washed and trimmed
$^1/_2$ teaspoon freshly ground black pepper

1 Place the mung beans, water and salt in a large saucepan and bring to a boil for 30 minutes or until the beans are tender. Drain the beans and set aside.
2 In another large saucepan, heat the oil and brown the pork. Drain and set the pork aside.
3 In the same saucepan, stir-fry the garlic until golden brown, then stir-fry the onion until translucent. Add the tomatoes and cook until they soften. Add the mung beans, stock and fermented shrimp, mix well and bring to a boil.
4 Reduce the heat and add the bitter melon leaves or spinach, and cook until just tender, about 3 minutes. Add the cooked pork, season with the pepper and stir to mix well. Serve hot.

Serves 4   Preparation time: 25 mins   Cooking time: 45 mins

Stuffed Eggplants Rellenong Talong

A popular eggplant dish with meat stuffing.

3 round or slender Asian eggplants
   (about 20 oz/600 g total)
3 eggs, beaten
3 1/2 tablespoons oil
4 cloves garlic, minced
1/2 large onion, diced
2 small tomatoes (about 9 oz/275 g
   total), diced
10 oz (300 g) ground pork or beef
1 teaspoon salt
1 teaspoon freshly ground black
   pepper
1/2 cup dried breadcrumbs
1 portion Balayan Fish Sauce (page 28)
   or Garlic Soy Vinegar Dip (page 29)

1 Prepare the Balayan Fish Sauce or Garlic Soy Vinegar Dip by following the instructions on pages 28 or 29.
2 Grill the eggplants for 30 minutes under a broiler, turning frequently to char the skins on all sides. The eggplants are ready when the skins are blackened and the flesh inside is soft. Remove from the heat and transfer to a work table. Holding the stem, slit one eggplant lengthwise so that the two halves are opened flat but still attached at the stem. Scoop out the pulp and set aside. Repeat with the other eggplants. Soak the skins in the beaten eggs and set aside.
3 For the stuffing, heat 2 tablespoons of the oil in a skillet and stir-fry the garlic until golden brown, add the onion and stir-fry until translucent. Then cook the tomatoes until they soften. Add the pork or beef and stir-fry for 5 minutes. Add the reserved eggplant pulp and season with the salt and pepper. Stir-fry the mixture until most of the liquid has evaporated, about 5 minutes. Remove from the heat.
4 Divide the stuffing mixture into 3 portions. Place each eggplant skin on a flat plate and press to flatten. Top each skin with 1 portion of the stuffing mixture, pressing it down firmly with a spatula, then sprinkle the breadcrumbs over it. Spoon the beaten egg over the breadcrumbs to cover the entire surface of the stuffing.
5 Heat 1/2 tablespoon of the oil in a skillet. Slide one of the stuffed eggplants into the skillet and cook for 1 minute. Then flip the eggplant over to cook the stuffing side for 3 minutes or until golden brown. Serve with small bowls of Balayan Fish Sauce or Garlic Soy Vinegar Dip on the side.

Serves 4–6   Preparation time: 25 mins   Cooking time: 30 mins

Vegetable Medley with Pork and Bagoong Pinakbet

This favorite dish of the Ilocanos in the north is flavored with pork and pungent *bagoong* or fermented shrimp.

2 tablespoons oil
2 cloves garlic, minced
1/2 medium onion, diced
12 oz (350 g) pork, cubed
2 1/2 in (6 cm) ginger, cubed
4 ripe tomatoes, diced
1 tablespoon fermented baby shrimp
   (*bagoong alamang*)
1/2 cup (125 ml) water
14 oz (400 g) Asian eggplants (about
   2–3 eggplants), cut into strips
3 small bitter melons (bitter gourd)
   (about 9 oz/275 g total)
   or 1 small zucchini, soft center and
   seeds discarded, cut into strips
6 okras (about 3 1/2 oz/100 g), caps
   discarded, stems halved
10 French beans, cut into lengths
Salt and black pepper, to taste

1 Heat the oil in a saucepan and stir-fry the garlic until golden brown, then stir-fry the onion until translucent. Add the pork and stir-fry over medium heat for 5–7 minutes, until browned.
2 Add the ginger and tomatoes, and stir-fry for another 5 minutes. Then, add the fermented shrimp and stir-fry for 3 minutes.
3 Add the water and bring to a boil. Reduce the heat and simmer for 15 minutes until the pork is tender. Add the eggplants, bitter melons, okras and beans, reduce the heat and allow to simmer for another 15 minutes. Season with salt and pepper if desired. Serve immediately.

Serves 4   Preparation time: 25 mins   Cooking time: 45 mins

Fresh Coconut Noodles with Vegetables
Pancit Buko

Fresh coconut is used instead of noodles in this reinterpretation of the traditional *pancit* by Lito Dalangin at the Villa Escudero.

1 tablespoon oil
3 cloves garlic, minced
$^1/_2$ medium onion, diced
$^1/_2$ cup (2 oz/60 g) boneless chicken, sliced
$^1/_2$ cup (2 oz/60 g) pork belly, sliced
$^1/_2$ cup (2 oz/60 g) green beans, sliced into lengths
$^1/_2$ small carrot, peeled and sliced into lengths
1 tablespoon fish sauce (*patis*)
  or $^1/_2$ teaspoon salt or more to taste
$^1/_4$ teaspoon freshly ground black pepper
$^1/_2$ cup (125 ml) Chicken Stock (page 28)
  or $^1/_4$ teaspoon chicken stock granules mixed with $^1/_2$ cup (125 ml) hot water
4 oz (125 g) fresh medium shrimp, shelled, deveined and halved lengthwise
1 cup (5 oz/150 g) fresh coconut meat, sliced into long, thin strips
2 leaves Chinese or Napa cabbage, thinly sliced (optional)
$^1/_2$ small green cabbage, thinly sliced
Kalamansi limes or regular limes, halved, to serve

1 Heat the oil in a saucepan and stir-fry the garlic until golden brown, then add the onion and stir-fry until translucent. Add the chicken and pork slices, and stir-fry until lightly browned, about 5 minutes.
2 Add the beans and carrot, and season with the fish sauce and pepper. Stir-fry briskly for a few seconds. Add the stock and shrimp, and bring to a boil. Cook until the shrimp turn pink and opaque, about 2 to 3 minutes.
3 Add the coconut strips and both types of cabbage, and cook until the vegetables are done but still crisp, about 2 minutes. Serve immediately with limes on the side.

Note: Fresh young coconut has a sweet soft flesh. Slice the young coconut meat into long thin strips to look like noodles. If using an older coconut, use a wooden spoon to scoop out the flesh and grate it into thin threads to achieve the same result. Or you can buy prepared young coconut strips, also known as *buko* strips in bottles or cans in Filipino grocery stores.

Serves 4–6   Preparation time: 35 mins   Cooking time: 15 mins

Bitter Melon Salad   Ensaladang Ampalaya

Bitter and salty flavors are blended together in this unique and highly nutritious salad from Vincent Yap at The Westin, Philippine Plaza. This salad makes a refreshing appetizer, although the bitterness of the melon and the strong flavor of the fermented baby shrimp (*bagoong alamang*) may take some getting used to for non-Filipinos.

4 small bitter melons (about 12 oz/350 g), deseeded and sliced
1 tablespoon salt
5 shallots, sliced
1 tablespoon fermented baby shrimp (*bagoong alamang*)
2 medium tomatoes, sliced
5 red bird's eye chilies (*siling labuyo*), sliced (optional)
1 tablespoon kalamansi lime juice or lemon juice

1 Sprinkle the bitter melons with the salt and place them in a colander for 30 minutes to drain. Rinse off the salt and dab the melon slices with paper towels to remove excess moisture.
2 In a large mixing bowl, toss the melon slices with the remaining ingredients. Allow to stand for 10 minutes to let the flavors develop, then serve.

Makes 4 cups   Preparation time: 20 mins

Green Mango Salad   Manggang Hilaw

A salad made with the unripened "Queen of Philippine Fruit".

2 medium unripe mangoes (about 1 lb/500 g), peeled and sliced
2 ripe tomatoes, sliced
1 hard-boiled salted egg (see note), cubed
5 shallots, sliced

1 Toss all the ingredients together and serve.

Note: To make **salted eggs**, place $3/4$ cup (12 tablespoons) salt into a pan, add a dozen eggs in the shell and enough water to cover. Boil for 2 minutes, then transfer the eggs to sterilized jars and add the boiled salted water to fill the jar. Seal well and set aside for $1^1/_2$ months. Always cook the salted eggs before using. Salted eggs are available from Chinese supermarkets.

Serves 4–6   Preparation time: 15 mins

Simmered Vegetables with Shrimp Guisadong Gulay

A simple but delicious way to cook a selection of fresh vegetables with shrimp and other meats.

8 oz (250 g) boneless pork loin
3 cups (750 ml) water
3 tablespoons oil
6 cloves garlic, minced
$1/2$ medium onion, diced
2 small tomatoes, diced
1 tablespoon fish sauce (*patis*)
  or $3/4$ teaspoon salt
$1/4$ teaspoon freshly ground black
  pepper
1 cup (100 g) cauliflower florets
1 small carrot, peeled and cut into
  bite-sized pieces
8 oz (250 g) fresh medium shrimp,
  shelled and deveined
1 cup (90 g) broccoli florets
$1/4$ small green cabbage, cut into
  bite-sized pieces
1 cup (5 oz/100 g) cooked fava
  beans or broad beans (optional)
1 cup ($3^1/2$ oz/100 g) snow peas, cut
into sections

1 In a deep saucepan, boil the pork in the water, uncovered, until the meat is cooked, about 10 minutes. Remove the meat, drain and set aside to cool. Strain and reserve $1^1/2$ cups (375 ml) of the stock. When the pork meat has cooled, cut it into 1-in ($2^1/2$-cm) cubes and set aside.
2 Heat the oil in a wok and stir-fry the garlic until golden brown, then add the onion and stir-fry until translucent. Add the tomatoes and cook until soft.
3 Add the pork cubes, reserved pork stock, fish sauce and pepper, and bring to a boil. Add the cauliflower and carrot, and cook for 3 minutes. Then add the shrimp and the rest of the vegetables, and cook for another 3 minutes, until the shrimp turn pink and the vegetables are cooked. Serve hot.

Serves 4–6   Preparation time: 35 mins   Cooking time: 45 mins

Taro Leaves with Coconut Milk Laing

A popular dish in the Bicol region where spicy foods are common. It is believed that taro leaves should be placed in a pot and not stirred. Instead, they should be simmered gently, as stirring would cause the leaves to be very tart, meaning the leaves would bite the tongue. Chard or spinach make good substitutes.

1 lb (500 g) taro or spinach leaves,
  washed and trimmed
4 oz (125 g) boneless pork or chicken,
  diced
1 teaspoon minced ginger
$1^1/2$ cups (375 ml) thin coconut milk
  or $1/2$ cup (125 ml) coconut cream
  mixed with 1 cup (250 ml) water
2 oz (60 g) fresh shrimp, peeled,
  deveined and diced
$1/2$ tablespoon fermented baby
  shrimp (*bagoong alamang*)
2 finger-length green chilies (*siling
  mahaba*), washed and left whole
$1/2$ cup (125 ml) thick coconut milk
  or $1/4$ cup (60 ml) coconut cream
  mixed with $1/4$ cup (60 ml) water
$1/2$ teaspoon salt
$1/2$ teaspoon freshly ground black
  pepper

1 Slice the taro leaves or spinach coarsely into lengths and set aside.
2 Simmer the pork, ginger and thin coconut milk in a saucepan over low heat until the meat is cooked, about 7–10 minutes. Add the shrimp and fermented shrimp, and simmer for another 5 minutes.
3 Add the taro or spinach leaves, chilies and thick coconut milk, and simmer for 3 minutes or until the leaves are wilted and the oil separates from the milk. Season with the salt and pepper. Remove from the heat and serve immediately.

Serves 4   Preparation time: 15 mins   Cooking time: 15 mins

Fresh Spring Rolls Lumpiang Ubod

A dish that transcends various cultures. For a more informal gathering, place everything on the table and allow diners to create their own spring rolls.

Wrappers
3 eggs, beaten
2 tablespoons oil
1 cup (125 g) cornstarch
$1/2$ teaspoon salt
$1^1/_2$ cups (375 ml) water

Filling
3 tablespoons oil
2 cloves garlic, minced
$1/2$ medium onion, diced
2 cups heart of palm (about 10 oz/300 g), cut into thin slices,
  or 2 cups (10 oz/300 g) boiled bamboo shoots, cut into matchsticks
8 oz (250 g) fresh shrimp, shelled, deveined and minced
8 oz (250 g) boiled pork, cut into thin slices
1 cup (4 oz/125 g) very thinly sliced green beans
$3/_4$ teaspoon salt
$1/2$ teaspoon freshly ground black pepper
15 lettuce leaves, washed

Sauce
$1/_4$ cup (50 g) brown sugar
1 cup (250 ml) Chicken Stock (page 28) or $1/2$ teaspoon chicken stock granules
  mixed with 1 cup (250 ml) hot water
$1^1/_2$ tablespoons soy sauce
$3/_4$ teaspoon salt
$1/_4$ teaspoon freshly ground black pepper
1 tablespoon cornstarch
$1/2$ cup (3 oz/90 g) crushed peanuts, to garnish

1 To make the Wrappers, whisk the eggs into the oil. Then add the cornstarch and salt, and whisk until well dissolved. Add the water to form a smooth batter.
2 Ladle about 3 tablespoons of the batter onto a heated skillet and tilt the skillet so the batter forms a thin, even layer. Cook for 1 minute, then flip the Wrapper over and cook on the other side for another minute. Set the Wrapper aside. Repeat to make 14 more Wrappers or until the batter is used up.
3 To make the Filling, heat the oil in a saucepan and stir-fry the garlic until golden brown, then add the onion and stir-fry until translucent. Add the heart of palm or bamboo shoots and cook over medium heat until tender, about 5 minutes. Add the shrimp and pork, and cook until the shrimp turn pink. Add the green beans and simmer for 3 minutes. Season with the salt and pepper and mix well. Remove from the heat and set aside.
4 Combine all the Sauce ingredients, except the peanuts, in a deep saucepan or wok over high heat. Stir constantly until the sauce thickens, about 3 minutes. Remove from the heat and set aside to cool.
5 Lay a Wrapper on a flat surface. Place a lettuce leaf on the Wrapper, so that part of the leaf extends beyond the edge of the Wrapper. Place 3 tablespoons of the Filling at the edge of the Wrapper, then fold one end in and roll it up (see photo on opposite page).
6 Drizzle the Sauce over the spring rolls and sprinkle with the peanuts.

Makes 15 rolls   Preparation time: 30 mins   Cooking time: 35 mins

Fish Poached in Vinegar and Ginger Paksiw Na Isda

3 cloves garlic, peeled and crushed
2 in (5 cm) fresh ginger, sliced
$\frac{1}{2}$ teaspoon black peppercorns,
  cracked
$1\frac{1}{3}$ cups (325 ml) water
$\frac{1}{2}$ cup (125 ml) Filipino vinegar
  (*suka*) or apple cider vinegar
1 teaspoon fish sauce (*patis*)
  or $\frac{1}{2}$ teaspoon salt
2 finger-length green chilies (*siling
  mahaba*)
1 whole fish, cleaned and scaled, or
  4 fish fillets (about 1 lb/500 g total)
  (sea bass, red snapper or mullet)
1 tablespoon oil
2 spring onions, thinly sliced,
  to garnish

1 Bring the garlic, ginger, peppercorns, water and vinegar to a boil in a clay, enamel or non-reactive pot. Add the fish sauce and chilies, and simmer for 3 minutes.
2 Add the fish and oil and simmer, covered, until the fish is cooked, about 10 minutes. Garnish with freshly sliced spring onions and serve immediately.

Serves 4   Preparation time: 15 mins   Cooking time: 20 mins

Shrimp Adobo in Coconut Milk Adobong Hipon Sa Gata

A variation of *adobo* popular in the Bicol region which uses coconut milk.

1 lb (500 g) fresh medium shrimp,
  shells intact
One 12-oz (350-ml) can thick coconut
  milk or $\frac{3}{4}$ cup (175 ml) coconut
  cream mixed with $\frac{3}{4}$ cup (175 ml)
  water
3 cloves garlic, thinly sliced and fried
  until crisp, to garnish (optional)
Kamias (see note) limes, sliced, to
  serve (optional)

Marinade
$\frac{1}{2}$ cup (125 ml) Filipino vinegar
  (*suka*) or apple cider vinegar
$\frac{1}{4}$ cup (60 ml) water
Pinch of freshly ground black pepper
2 cloves garlic, minced
1 teaspoon fish sauce (*patis*)
  or $\frac{1}{4}$ teaspoon salt

1 Combine the Marinade ingredients in a saucepan, place the shrimp in the pan and coat well, then set in the refrigerator to marinate for 1 hour. Remove the shrimp and bring the Marinade to a boil. Cook, uncovered, for 5 minutes.
2 Reduce the heat, add the coconut milk and simmer for 15 minutes to allow the sauce to thicken. Return the shrimp to the pot, stir and bring to a boil. Immediately, remove from the heat and garnish with the fried garlic. Serve hot with the *kamias* limes on the side.

Note: *Kamias* are related to starfruit. They are small, cylindrical, yellow-green fruits with a sour, acidic juice usually used as a souring agent.

Serves 4   Preparation time: 15 mins + marinate 1 hour   Cooking time: 25 mins

Sweet and Sour Fish Escabeche

A popular Spanish-Chinese dish, adapted by the Filipinos using local ingredients.

1 red snapper, grouper, sea bass or
  carp (about 1 lb/500 g), cleaned
  and left whole
4 teaspoons salt
$^1/_3$ cup (90 ml) Filipino vinegar (*suka*)
  or apple cider vinegar
$^1/_2$ cup (125 ml) water
$^1/_2$ cup (100 g) brown sugar
4 tablespoons oil
4 cloves garlic, minced
1 medium onion, diced
2 in (5 cm) ginger, sliced
$^1/_2$ bell pepper, deseeded and cut
  into matchsticks
$^1/_2$ stick celery, cut into matchsticks
$^1/_2$ small carrot, cut into matchsticks
2 spring onions, cut into lengths and
  sliced lengthwise into strips
1 tablespoon cornstarch

1 Clean the fish and slit it open. Season the fish all over with 1 tablespoon of the salt.

2 Whisk the vinegar, water, sugar and the remaining salt in a small non-reactive bowl until the sugar and salt have dissolved. Set aside.

3 Heat the oil in a skillet and fry the fish until crisp and light golden brown, about 7 minutes on each side. Remove the fish from the skillet and set aside to drain.

4 In the same skillet, stir-fry the garlic until golden brown, then add the onion and stir-fry until translucent. Add the ginger and the vinegar mixture and bring to a boil. Add the bell pepper, celery, carrot and spring onions, and mix well. Add the cornstarch and stir to dissolve. Reduce the heat and simmer for 5 minutes or until the sauce thickens.

5 Transfer the fish to a serving platter and spoon the cooked vegetables over it. Serve hot with a small bowl of the sauce on the side.

Serves 4   Preparation time: 25 mins   Cooking time: 30 mins

Fried Fish with Black Bean Sauce
Lapu Lapu Sa Tausi

A Chinese-influenced dish with a delicious sauce of ginger and salted black beans. Just like *bagoong*, salted black beans are an acquired taste.

1 grouper or red snapper (about 1 lb/500 g), cleaned, scaled and left whole
$1/_2$ teaspoon salt
$1/_4$ teaspoon freshly ground black pepper
$1/_4$ cup (60 ml) oil
4 tablespoons cornstarch dissolved in 6 tablespoons water
1 teaspoon sesame oil
Spring onion, thinly sliced, to garnish

Black Bean Sauce
1 small cake pressed tofu (about 5 oz/150 g), drained and diced
6 cloves garlic, minced
1 in ($2^1/_2$ cm) ginger, minced
2–3 tablespoons salted whole black beans, lightly mashed
$1^1/_2$ cups (375 ml) water
3 shallots, diced
3 small tomatoes, cut into wedges
1 tablespoon cornstarch dissolved in 4 tablespoons water

1 Season the fish with the salt and pepper. Heat the oil in a skillet large enough to hold the fish. Dip the seasoned fish in the cornstarch-water mixture and fry in the hot oil until crisp and golden brown, about 5 minutes on each side. Drain on paper towels and set aside.
2 Reserve 3 tablespoons of the oil in the skillet and drain away the rest. Make the Black Bean Sauce by frying the tofu lightly in the skillet for 3 minutes until golden brown. Add the minced garlic and ginger, and stir-fry lightly for a minute. Then add the black beans and water, and stir to mix well. Add the shallots and tomatoes. Bring the mixture to a boil, then lower the heat and simmer for 5 minutes. Add the cornstarch mixture and stir for 1 to 2 minutes until it thickens. Remove from the heat.
3 Transfer the fish to a serving platter and ladle the sauce over it. Just before serving, drizzle the sesame oil over the fish and garnish with freshly sliced spring onion. Best served hot.

Serves 4   Preparation time: 35 mins   Cooking time: 25 mins

Shrimp Sinigang   Sour Shrimp Soup

Sinigang uses sour ingredients such as tamarind or lemon to create a deliciously tart and spicy broth.

8 cups (2 liters) rice water or water
1/2 cup (125 ml) kalamansi lime juice or lemon juice
2 tablespoons oil
2 cloves garlic, minced
1/2 medium onion, diced
2 large ripe tomatoes, diced
1 cup (200 g) daikon radish, peeled and sliced
1 lb (500 g) fresh medium shrimp, shells intact
3 finger-length green chilies (*siling mahaba*)
1 1/2 lbs (750 g) watercress, spinach or water spinach, washed and trimmed
1 tablespoon fish sauce (*patis*) or 1 teaspoon salt
1/2 teaspoon freshly ground black pepper

1 Bring the rice water and lime juice or lemon juice to a boil in a saucepan. Reduce the heat and simmer for 15 minutes.
2 In the meantime, heat the oil in a skillet and stir-fry the garlic until golden brown, then stir-fry the onion until translucent. Add the tomatoes and cook until they soften. Add this fried mixture to the saucepan with the rice water.
3 Add the daikon radish and bring to a boil again. Reduce the heat and simmer until the daikon is tender but still crisp, about 7 minutes.
4 Add the shrimp, chilies and watercress, and cook until the shrimp turn pink and the vegetables are wilted, about 5 minutes. Season with the fish sauce and pepper.
5 Ladle the stew into a large bowl and serve immediately with boiled rice.

Note: To prepare rice water for this recipe, mix 8 cups (2 liters) water with 4 cups (800 g) uncooked rice. Stir and strain, reserving the rice water.

Serves 4–6   Preparation time: 25 mins   Cooking time: 30 mins

Fish Soup with Vegetables   Pesang Dalag

The success of this simple fish soup depends on the freshness of the fish and the ginger.

3 cups (750 ml) rice water or water
2 in (5 cm) fresh ginger, thinly sliced
1/2 teaspoon peppercorns, cracked
1 onion, quartered
1/2 small green cabbage, quartered
2 teaspoons oil
1/2 teaspoon salt
1 tablespoon fish sauce (*patis*)
Freshly ground black pepper, to taste
1 1/2 lbs (750 g) fresh fish fillets (catfish, grouper or tilapia), cut into serving slices
1 bunch lettuce or leafy greens, cut into pieces (optional)
1 baby leek or 2 spring onions, sliced, to garnish
1 portion Miso Tomato Sauce (page 25)

1 Prepare the Miso Tomato Sauce by following the instructions on page 25.
2 Boil the rice water, ginger and peppercorns for 5 minutes. Add the onion and cabbage, and simmer for 3 minutes.
3 Add the oil, salt, fish sauce and ground pepper, and boil for another 2 minutes. Reduce the heat, add the fish and green vegetables, and simmer for 10 minutes.
4 Ladle the stew into a large serving bowl, garnish with leek or spring onions and serve with the Miso Tomato Sauce on the side.

Note: To prepare rice water for this recipe, mix 3 cups (750 ml) water with 1 cup (200 g) uncooked rice. Stir and strain, reserving the rice water.

Serves 4   Preparation time: 20 mins   Cooking time: 20 mins

Rich Beef Stew Caldereta

Caldereta, another Filipino dish tracing its roots to Spain, is a rich stew made of beef stir-fried in olive oil and simmered to perfection in a tomato sauce. Originally, goat meat was used for this dish, but nowadays, beef, pork or chicken are used.

1/4 cup (60 ml) olive oil
6 cloves garlic, minced
2 medium onions, diced
1 1/2 cups (125 g) diced fresh tomatoes or one 14-oz (400-g) can peeled tomatoes
1 bell pepper, deseeded and thinly sliced
1 lb (500 g) beef sirloin, cubed
4 oz (125 g) beef liver, cubed
2–3 cups (500–750 ml) beef stock or 1 teaspoon beef stock granules mixed with 2–3 cups (500–750 ml) hot water
1 tablespoon tomato paste
1 teaspoon freshly ground black pepper
1/2 cup (50 g) green olives
1–2 dill pickles, cubed
3–4 finger-length chilies (*siling maha-ba*), sliced
1/2 cup (125 ml) whipping cream
1/2 cup (1 1/2 oz/50 g) grated Parmesan cheese
1 red bell pepper or pimento, cut into strips, to garnish (optional)

1 Heat the oil in a saucepan and stir-fry the garlic until golden brown, then stir-fry the onions until translucent. Add the tomatoes and bell pepper, and cook until they soften. Add the beef and liver, and stir-fry for a few minutes. When the liver is cooked, remove it from the saucepan and set aside in a small bowl.
2 Add the beef stock and tomato paste, and simmer over low heat until the beef is tender, about 45 minutes. Season with the pepper.
3 Add the olives, dill pickles and chilies. Mash the liver with a fork and return to the saucepan.
4 Cook until the sauce thickens, about 5 to 7 minutes, then add the cream and cheese, and mix well. Remove from the heat, transfer to a platter and garnish with the bell pepper or pimento strips.

Serves 4   Preparation time: 30 mins   Cooking time: 1 hour

Filipino-style Beef Steak Bistek

1 1/2 lbs (750 g) beef sirloin or skirt steak, cut into thin fillets
2 tablespoons kalamansi lime juice or lemon juice
2 tablespoons soy sauce
2 teaspoons freshly ground black pepper
3 tablespoons oil
1 medium onion, sliced into rings
Salt to taste

1 Marinate the beef slices in the kalamansi lime juice, soy sauce and pepper overnight in the refrigerator.
2 Heat the oil in a skillet and pan-fry the beef until medium-rare, about 30 seconds on each side. Transfer the beef slices to a plate.
3 In the remaining oil, stir-fry the onion until it is browned. Season the beef with a sprinkling of salt and drizzle a little of the pan juice over the steak. Garnish with the onion slices and serve.

Serves 4   Preparation time: 10 mins + overnight marination   Cooking time: 10 mins

Stuffed Beef Roll   Morcon

This delicious dish inherited from Spain is a must for the fiesta table. The meat roll is simmered in a rich tomato sauce until juicy and tender.

$1^1/_2$ lbs (750 g) beef flank steak, cut into large sheets about $^1/_2$ in (1 cm) thick
2 tablespoons lemon juice
4 tablespoons soy sauce
1 teaspoon freshly ground black pepper
Kitchen string
3–4 tablespoons olive oil
5 cloves garlic, peeled and crushed
1 onion, diced
1 cup (250 ml) tomato purée
2 bay leaves
3 cups (750 ml) beef stock or water
$^3/_4$ teaspoon salt
1 teaspoon freshly ground black pepper
1 teaspoon sugar
2 tablespoons lemon juice
1 bunch parsley (optional), to garnish

Filling
5 canned Vienna sausages, sliced into strips lengthwise
1 small carrot, quartered lengthwise
4 strips bacon
2 hard-boiled eggs, quartered lengthwise
2 tablespoons diced sweet pickles or relish
3 slices sharp Cheddar cheese

1 Marinate the beef for 20 minutes in the lemon juice, soy sauce and pepper. Drain and reserve the marinade.
2 Lay the beef on a flat work surface. Arrange the Filling in rows lengthwise. Roll the meat lengthwise along the grain to enclose the Filling and tie in several places with kitchen string. Then dredge the meat roll in flour and shake to remove excess flour.
3 Heat the oil in a large saucepan and brown the beef on all sides. Remove the meat from the saucepan and set aside. Add the reserved marinade, garlic, onion, tomato purée and bay leaves, and cook over high heat until the liquid is reduced. Add the beef stock and bring to a boil.
4 Add the beef roll, reduce the heat and cook on a slow simmer for 1 hour or until the meat is tender. Season with salt, pepper and sugar.
5 Transfer the meat roll to a platter, remove the string and slice crosswise into $^3/_4$-in ($1^1/_2$-cm) thick slices. Reheat the gravy and drizzle over the meat just before serving. Freshen the dish with the lemon juice and garnish with parsley, if using.

Note: Marinating the beef overnight helps to improve the flavor of the dish.

Serves 6   Preparation time: 20 mins   Cooking time: 1 hour 10 mins

Oxtail and Vegetable Stew Kare-Kare

This native Filipino oxtail and vegetable stew is flavored with ground rice and peanuts.

3–4 lbs (1$\frac{1}{2}$–2 kg) oxtail, cut into serving pieces

8 cups (2 liters) water

$\frac{1}{2}$ cup (100 g) uncooked rice grains, ground to a powder in a food processor or blender

4 tablespoons oil

4 cloves garlic, minced

2 small onions, diced

1$\frac{1}{2}$ cups (375 ml) Annatto Water (page 29)

$\frac{1}{2}$ cup (90 g) roasted unsalted peanuts, ground or 3 tablespoons peanut butter

2 slender Asian eggplants (about 14 oz/400 g), cut into chunks

10 green beans, cut into lengths

1 small Chinese or Napa cabbage, washed and quartered

2 teaspoons salt

1 teaspoon freshly ground black pepper

1 teaspoon brown sugar

2 teaspoons kalamansi lime juice or lemon juice

1 Boil the oxtail in the water for 2 hours or until tender. Drain the meat and set aside. Strain and reserve 4 cups (1 liter) of the stock.

2 Dry-fry the rice power in a skillet over low heat, stirring constantly for 5 to 7 minutes until the powder is lightly browned. Remove from the heat and set aside.

3 Heat the oil in a large saucepan and stir-fry the garlic until golden brown, then stir-fry the onions until translucent. Add the Annatto Water and oxtail to the saucepan and bring to a boil.

4 Add the roasted rice powder, peanuts or peanut butter and reserved stock along with the eggplants, green beans and cabbage, and mix well. Bring the stew to a boil, reduce the heat and simmer for 10 minutes. Season with the salt and pepper.

5 Add the brown sugar and lime juice and stir to mix well. Serve with a small bowl of sautéed fermented baby shrimp (*bagoong alamang*).

Serves 8   Preparation time: 20 mins   Cooking time: 1 hour 20 mins

Pork with Bagoong Binagoongang Baboy

2 tablespoons oil

5 cloves garlic, minced

1 small onion, diced

1 small tomato, diced

1$\frac{1}{2}$ lbs (750 g) boneless pork shoulder or rump, cubed

$\frac{1}{2}$ teaspoon sugar

$\frac{3}{4}$ cup (175 ml) water

4 tablespoons fermented baby shrimp (*bagoong alamang*)

6–8 green bird's eye chilies (*siling labuyo*), lightly bruised (optional)

1 Heat the oil in a large skillet and stir-fry the garlic until golden brown, then stir-fry the onion until translucent. Add the tomato and cook until soft.

2 Add the pork and sugar, and cook over medium heat until the meat is browned, about 10 minutes. Add the water and simmer, covered, for 30 minutes until the pork is cooked.

3 Add the fermented shrimp and chilies, and simmer for another 15 minutes or until the pork is very tender. Stir occasionally to prevent the sauce from burning. Best served hot with white rice.

Serves 4–6   Preparation time: 15 mins   Cooking time: 1 hour

Beef Sinigang   Beef and Vegetable Tamarind Stew

Sinigang, the quintessential Filipino dish, consists of any type of meat or seafood prepared in a delicious spicy stew with vegetables and a fragrant tamarind gravy.

4 cups (1 liter) water
1 lb (500 g) beef ribs or stewing beef, cut into pieces
4 small tomatoes, sliced or one 10-oz (300-g) can peeled tomatoes
4 finger-length green chilies (*siling mahaba*), whole
1 small onion, sliced
2 heaped tablespoons tamarind pulp mixed with 1 cup (250 ml) warm water, mashed and strained to obtain juice
3 potatoes (14 oz/400 g), peeled and cut into chunks
7 oz (200 g) green beans, cut into lengths
1 lb (500 g) water spinach, washed and trimmed, leaves and stalks separated, stalks cut into lengths or 8 oz (250 g) spinach leaves, washed
1 tablespoon fish sauce (*patis*) or 1 teaspoon salt
Freshly ground black pepper, to taste

1 Bring the water to a boil in a saucepan. Add the beef, tomatoes, chilies, onion and tamarind juice, and simmer for 20 minutes.
2 Add the potato chunks and simmer for another 25 minutes. When the potatoes are tender, add the green beans and spinach stalks and cook for 3 minutes. Season with the fish sauce or salt and a pinch of pepper.
3 Add the spinach leaves and cook for another 3 minutes until the leaves are wilted. Serve hot with freshly steamed rice.

Serves 4   Preparation time: 25 mins   Cooking time: 45 mins

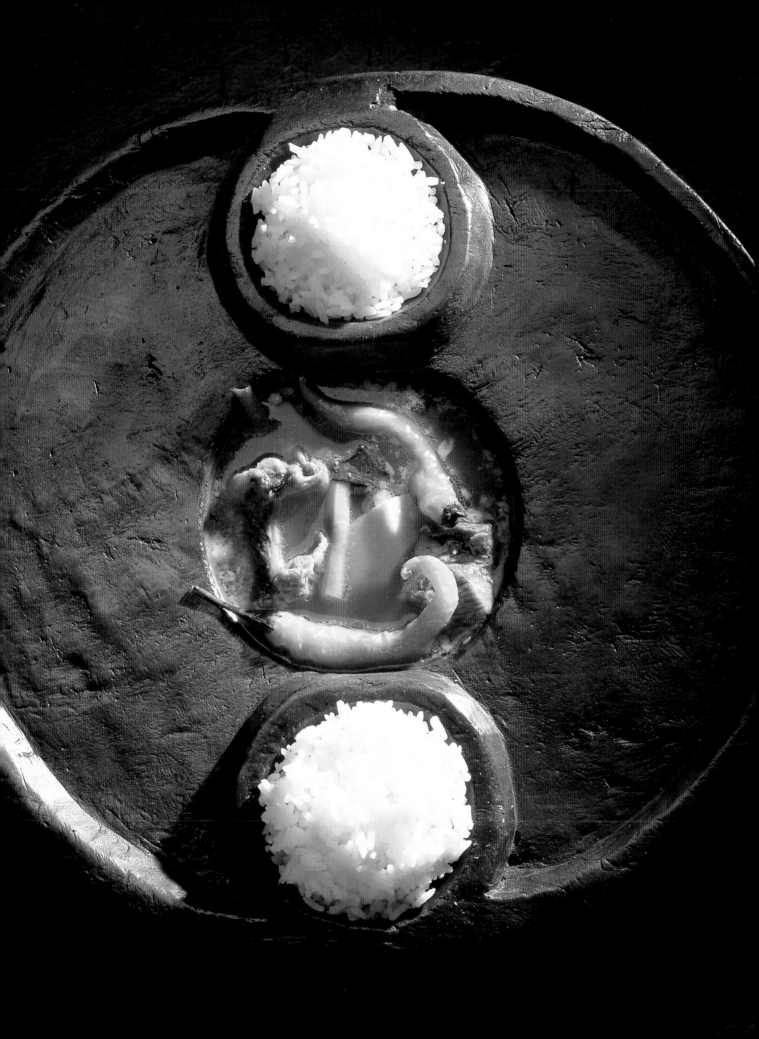

Beef Braised with Garlic and Olives   Lengua Estofado

A product of strong Iberian influence, this fiesta dish is usually cooked with beef tongue—a prized cut of meat—braised in wine, spices and vinegar.

20 oz (600 g) beef shin or tongue
3 tablespoons oil
3 tablespoons minced garlic
1/2 onion, diced
1 tomato, diced
2 potatoes, peeled and sliced
2 carrots (8 oz/250 g), sliced
Salt and black pepper, to taste
1/3 cup (30 g) stuffed olives
5 button mushrooms, halved (optional)
2–3 small plantains or unripe
  bananas, halved and fried (optional)

Marinade
1/2 cup (125 ml) water
1/2 teaspoon peppercorns, cracked
1 bay leaf
1 1/2 tablespoons apple cider vinegar
  or 2 tablespoons white wine or sherry
1 tablespoon soy sauce
1 tablespoon sugar
1 teaspoon salt

1 Boil the beef in a large pot of water for 15 minutes. Drain the meat. Combine the Marinade ingredients with the beef and set aside to marinate for 40 minutes. Then heat the oil in a large pot and brown the beef on all sides, reserving the marinade in a bowl. Remove the beef from the pot and set aside.
2 In the same pot, stir-fry the garlic until golden brown, then stir-fry the onion until translucent. Add the tomato and stir-fry until soft. Return the beef and the reserved marinade to the pot and simmer for 1 hour or until the beef is tender. Add water as needed and prick the beef with a fork to allow the juices to penetrate into the meat (a pressure cooker may be used to reduce the cooking time).
3 Remove the beef and slice into serving portions. Return the sliced beef to the pot, add the potatoes and carrots, and simmer until the vegetables are tender, about 10 minutes. Season with salt and pepper.
4 Add the stuffed olives and mushrooms, if using, and simmer for another 5 minutes. Serve hot with the fried plantains if desired.

Serves 4–6   Preparation time: 15 mins   Cooking time: 1 hour 10 mins

Crispy Roast Pork   Lechon Kawali

The ubiquitous *lechon*, quintessential fiesta fare, has a wonderfully crisp skin.

1¹/₂–2 lbs (³/₄–1 kg) pork belly or
  pork ribs, with skin left on
10 cloves garlic, peeled and crushed
1 teaspoon salt
1 tablespoon freshly ground black
  pepper
10 cups (2¹/₂ liters) water
Oil for brushing
1 portion Liver Sauce (page 28)

1 Prepare the Liver Sauce by following the instructions on page 28.
2 Slice the pork belly or pork ribs into 4 pieces, about ³/₄ in (2 cm) thick.
Season the meat with the garlic, salt and pepper. Boil the seasoned meat in
the water in a large pot until tender, about 1 hour. Drain on a wire rack and
allow to stand for another hour.
3 Brush the pork skin with the oil and bake in a preheated oven at 425°F
(220°C) for 20 minutes, brushing the skin with oil every 10 minutes.
(Alternatively, you may deep-fry the pork in hot oil until the skin is crisp.) Then
slice the meat and serve with a small bowl of the Liver Sauce on the side.

Serves 4   Preparation time: 20 mins   Cooking time: 1 hour 20 mins

Tripe, Pork and Sausage with Chickpeas in Gravy   Callos

Beef tripe or stomach is a delicacy in many countries and is available from butcher shops or Asian food stores. If you cannot get it, simply increase the amount of pork used or add some other meat instead.

2 lbs (1 kg) beef tripe, rinsed
1 lb (500 g) boneless pork leg, cubed
2 in (5 cm) fresh ginger, sliced
3 cups (750 ml) water mixed with
  3 tablespoons salt
5 strips bacon
2 potatoes, peeled and cut into thick
  slices
3 *chorizos de Bilbao* or other spicy
  sausage like pepperoni, sliced into
  rounds
1 cup (7 oz/200 g) cooked or canned
  chickpeas
One 8-oz (250-g) can puréed tomato
2 cups (500 ml) water
Salt and black pepper, to taste
3 tablespoons diced pimento or bell
  pepper
1 cup (250 ml) tomato ketchup
1 green or red bell pepper, deseeded
  and cut into strips

1 Boil the tripe, pork and ginger in the salted water until tender, about 40–45 minutes (use a pressure cooker to save time). Drain and rinse the tripe, and cut it into 1-in (2^1/$_2$-cm) squares. Drain the pork, allow it to cool and cut away the fat from the meat. Set aside and discard the fat.

2 In a large skillet, fry the bacon and allow the fat to render, then remove the bacon strips and drain on paper towels. In the same skillet, fry the potatoes, *chorizos* or pepperoni and chickpeas in the bacon fat. Add the tomato purée, fried bacon, cooked tripe and pork, and the water. Stir and simmer, covered, over low heat for 20 minutes. Season with salt and pepper.

3 Add the pimento, tomato ketchup and bell pepper, and a little water if the mixture is too dry, and stir to blend the flavors. Serve hot with rice.

Serves 6–8   Preparation time: 30 mins   Cooking time: 1 hour

Hearty Meat Stew with Chickpeas and Plantains   Pochero

Lynn Sunico of Manila's Skyline Restaurant has provided her immensely popular and delicious recipe for a version of the Spanish *cocido*, a favorite Sunday meal in the Philippines. This recipe includes chickpeas and plantains or *saging na saba*.

10 oz (300 g) pork belly or shoulder, cut into bite-sized pieces
10 oz (300 g) chicken, cut into bite-sized pieces
10 oz (300 g) boneless beef shank, cut into bite-sized pieces
Two 3-in (8-cm) pieces of *chorizos de Bilbao* or pepperoni sausage, cut into bite-sized pieces
4 cups (1 liter) water or beef stock
1 teaspoon salt
1 spring onion, thinly sliced
2 tablespoons olive oil
3 cloves garlic, minced
1 medium onion, diced
2 cups (500 g) diced tomatoes or one 16-oz (450 g) can peeled tomatoes
4 tablespoons tomato paste
1 small green cabbage, quartered (optional)
8 oz (250 g) green beans
2 small plantains, quartered (optional)
3 small potatoes (about 10 oz/300 g), peeled, halved and deep-fried
1 cup (7 oz/200 g) cooked chickpeas, drained if using canned chickpeas
1 teaspoon salt
1 teaspoon freshly ground black pepper
1 portion Eggplant Sauce (page 29)

1 Prepare the Eggplant Sauce by following the instructions on page 29.
2 Place the meat and sausages in a large pot with the water, salt and spring onion, and bring to a boil. Reduce the heat and simmer, uncovered, over medium to low heat until the meat is tender, about 45 minutes. Drain the meat and sausages, and set aside. Reserve the stock.
3 Heat the oil in a pot and stir-fry the garlic until golden brown, then stir-fry the onion until translucent. Add the tomatoes and tomato paste, and cook until soft, about 5 minutes.
4 Add the reserved stock and bring to a boil. Add the cabbage, green beans and plantains, and cook for another 5 minutes. Add the meat and sausages, potatoes and chickpeas. Season with the salt and pepper, and simmer for a few minutes. Serve with a bowl of the Eggplant Sauce on the side.

Serves 6–8   Preparation time: 30 mins   Cooking time: 55 mins

Stewed Pork Knuckle Paksiw Na Pata

This piquant dish with soy sauce, sugar and bay leaves is another national favorite.

1 large pork knuckle (about 2 lbs/1 kg)
8 cups (2 liters) water
1/2 cup (125 ml) Filipino vinegar
  (*suka*) or apple cider vinegar
1/4 cup (60 ml) black soy sauce
1/3 cup (60 g) brown sugar
3 bay leaves
5 cloves garlic, peeled and crushed
1/2 cup (35 g) dried banana heart or
  lily buds, rinsed and soaked in
  water until soft, or 2 cups (200 g)
  cabbage, coarsely chopped
1/2 teaspoon salt
1/2 teaspoon freshly ground black
  pepper

1 Place the pork in a large saucepan with the water, cover, and bring to a boil. Add the vinegar, soy sauce, brown sugar, bay leaves and garlic, reduce the heat and simmer until the pork is tender and the sauce has thickened, about 45 minutes.
2 Add the banana heart and simmer for another 30 minutes. Season with the salt and pepper, and serve immediately.

Serves 4   Preparation time: 15 mins   Cooking time: 1 hour 15 mins

Pork Stew with Tahure Humba

A Chinese-influenced dish slowly simmered in a pot to bring out its melt-in-the-mouth texture.

2 lbs (1 kg) pork collar, cut into serving pieces
4 cups (1 liter) water
Two 2-in (5-cm) blocks *tahure* (about
  1 oz/30 g), mashed
1/3 cup (2 oz/60 g) toasted unsalted
  peanuts, coarsely chopped (optional)
Salt to taste

Marinade
1 cup (250 ml) Filipino vinegar (*suka*)
  or apple cider vinegar
2 tablespoons soy sauce
2 cloves garlic, peeled and crushed
1/2 teaspoon dried oregano
1/3 cup (60 g) brown sugar
1 tablespoon peppercorns, cracked
1 bay leaf

1 Mix the Marinade ingredients together in a heavy saucepan, add the pork and marinate for at least 2 hours or overnight.
2 Add the water and bring to a boil. Reduce the heat and simmer until the pork is tender, about 45 minutes to an hour.
3 Add the *tahure* and peanuts, if using, stir and cook until the sauce thickens, about 5 minutes. Season with salt and serve hot.

Note: *Tahure*, a type of fermented paste made from black and yellow soybeans, is sold in cans and small bottles in Filipino grocery stores. Substitute dark miso or black bean sauce.

Serves 4   Preparation time: 20 mins + 2 hours marination
Cooking time: 1 hour

Grilled Garlic Vinegar Pork   Inihaw Na Baboy

Inihaw or grilling is one of the basic Filipino cooking techniques and this simple dish works beautifully because of the marination in garlic and vinegar.

8 pork chops or pork steaks (about
   2¹/₂ lbs/1¹/₄ kg)
5 cloves garlic, peeled and crushed
¹/₂ cup (125 ml) Filipino vinegar
   (*suka*) or apple cider vinegar
¹/₂ cup (125 ml) soy sauce
1 tablespoon freshly ground black
   pepper
1 portion Garlic Soy Vinegar Dip
   (page 29) or Sweet and Sour Sauce
   (page 25)

1 Marinate the pork in the garlic, vinegar, soy sauce and pepper overnight in the refrigerator.
2 Prepare the Garlic Soy Vinegar Dip or Sweet and Sour Sauce by following the instructions on page 29 or 25.
3 Grill the meat over red-hot charcoal or under the broiler and serve with small bowls of the dip on the side.

Serves 4   Preparation time: 5 mins + overnight marination   Cooking time: 10 mins

Diced Pork and Liver Stew with Potatoes and Pimentos   Menudo

Menudo, an adaptation from the Spanish word meaning "tiny", refers to a humble, everyday dish of slow-simmered pieces of diced meat mixed with potatoes.

8 oz (250 g) pork loin, diced
1 cup (250 ml) water
2 tablespoons oil
4 cloves garlic, minced
1 onion, diced
2 tomatoes, diced
³/₄ cup (175 ml) tomato paste
5 oz (150 g) pork liver, diced
1 bay leaf
1 large or 2 medium potatoes (7 oz/
   200 g total), cubed
2 teaspoons fish sauce (*patis*)
   or ¹/₂ teaspoon salt
¹/₂ teaspoon freshly ground black
   pepper
¹/₂ cup (75 g) diced pimento or 1 large
   red bell pepper, deseeded and diced
¹/₃ cup (60 g) cooked chickpeas or
   peas

1 In a small pot, boil the pork in the water for 10 minutes until tender. Skim the foam off the surface, drain the pork and set aside. Then strain and reserve ¹/₂ cup (125 ml) of the stock.
2 Heat the oil in a skillet and stir-fry the garlic until golden brown, then add the onion and stir-fry until translucent. Add the tomatoes and tomato paste, and cook until soft. Add the pork, liver and bay leaf, and cook for another 5 minutes. Add the reserved pork stock and potato, and simmer for 10 minutes until the potato is soft. Season with the fish sauce and pepper.
3 Add the pimento or bell pepper and chickpeas, and simmer for another 10 minutes. Remove from the heat and serve immediately.

Serves 4   Preparation time: 20 mins   Cooking time: 35 mins

Chicken Adobo with Turmeric and Coconut Milk   Adobong Manok

Adobo, meaning cooked in vinegar and garlic, is the national dish of the Philippines. This *adobo* is enriched with coconut milk and turmeric.

1 chicken (2 lbs/1 kg), cut into
  serving pieces
1 tablespoon oil
1 cup (250 ml) thick coconut milk
  or 1/2 cup (125 ml) coconut cream
  mixed with 1/2 cup (125 ml) water
2–4 finger-length green chilies (*siling mahaba*), whole
1/2 tablespoon fish sauce (*patis*)

Marinade
1 tablespoon grated fresh turmeric
  root or 11/2 teaspoons turmeric
  powder
10 cloves garlic, minced
1/4 cup (60 ml) Filipino vinegar (*suka*)
  or apple cider vinegar
1/2 teaspoon salt
1/4 teaspoon freshly ground black
  pepper

1 Combine the Marinade ingredients in a large bowl, add the chicken and mix well. Marinate the chicken overnight in the refrigerator. Drain the chicken and reserve the Marinade.
2 Heat the oil in a saucepan and stir-fry the marinated chicken until lightly browned, about 5 minutes.
3 Add the reserved Marinade and the coconut milk or cream, and simmer, uncovered, over low heat until the sauce thickens and the oil separates from the milk, about 30 minutes. Add the chilies and season with the fish sauce. Stir to mix well and serve immediately.

Serves 4–6   Preparation time: 25 mins + overnight marination
Cooking time: 30 mins

Chicken Simmered in Tomatoes and Pimentos   Apritadang Manok

2 tablespoons olive oil
1 chicken (2 lbs/1 kg), cut into serving
  pieces
2 cloves garlic, peeled and crushed
1 large onion, diced
1 lb (500 g) ripe tomatoes, diced
  or one 14-oz (400-g) can whole
  peeled tomatoes, diced
2 bay leaves
1 teaspoon salt or to taste
1/2–1 tablespoon freshly ground
  black pepper
11/2 cups (375 ml) water
2 large potatoes, peeled and cubed
1 cup (125 g) pimentos, drained or
  1 large red bell pepper, deseeded
  and diced

1 Heat the oil in a large saucepan and lightly brown the chicken. Remove the chicken and set aside. Add the garlic and stir-fry until golden brown, then stir-fry the onion until translucent. Return the chicken to the saucepan, add the tomatoes, bay leaves, salt, pepper and water, and simmer over low heat for 20 minutes.
2 Add the potatoes and simmer for 15 minutes, then add the pimentos and simmer for another 5 minutes. Remove from the heat and serve immediately.

Serves 4   Preparation time: 25 mins   Cooking time: 35 mins

Chicken and Pork Adobo   Adobong Manok At Baboy

There are many versions of the ever-popular *adobo*; this one is from Joel Fabay at the Manila Hotel. It combines chicken and pork with vinegar and a hearty helping of garlic.

1 lb (500 g) pork, cut into chunks
1 bulb garlic, peeled and crushed
1 onion, diced
$^1/_2$ cup (125 ml) soy sauce
3 tablespoons Filipino vinegar (*suka*)
  or apple cider vinegar
1 teaspoon freshly ground black
  pepper
2 bay leaves
$1^1/_2$ cups (375 ml) water
8 oz (250 g) boneless chicken,
  cubed
1 portion Green Papaya Pickles
  (page 29)

1 Prepare the Green Papaya Pickles by following the instructions on page 29.
2 Combine the pork, garlic, onion, soy sauce, vinegar, pepper, bay leaves and water in a pot and bring to a boil. Reduce the heat and simmer until the pork is partially cooked, about 10 minutes.
3 Add the chicken and simmer for another 20 minutes, until both the pork and chicken are cooked. Remove from the heat and serve on a large platter with a bowl of the pickles on the side.

Serves 4–6   Preparation time: 20 mins   Cooking time: 35 mins

Stuffed Duck with Napa Cabbage   Rellenato De Pato

1 duck (about 4 lbs/2 kg), whole
1 tablespoon butter
1 teaspoon salt
1 teaspoon ground black pepper
Oil for deep-frying
9 cups (2$^1/_4$ liters) Chicken Stock
  (page 28) or 4$^1/_2$ teaspoons chicken
  stock granules mixed with 9 cups
  (2$^1/_4$ liters) hot water
1 leek, halved
2 bay leaves
$^1/_4$ cup (60 ml) sherry or brandy
1 whole Chinese or Napa cabbage,
  washed and sliced

Stuffing
2 onions, diced
5 button mushrooms, quartered
5 oz (150 g) ham, diced
10 oz (300 g) ground pork
1 tablespoon butter
2 eggs, beaten
1 cup fresh breadcrumbs

1 Make the Stuffing by sautéing the onions, mushrooms, ham and pork in the butter until the onions are soft and translucent. Strain the mixture, reserve the liquid and set the ingredients aside in a bowl to cool. When cooled, add the eggs and breadcrumbs, and mix well. Set aside.
2 Rinse the duck inside and out. Rub the butter, salt and pepper on the duck skin and inside its cavity. Then, stuff and truss the duck.
3 Heat the oil and deep-fry the duck until the skin is browned. Remove the duck from the oil and braise in a large pot with the reserved Stuffing liquid for 20 minutes.
4 Add the chicken stock, leek, bay leaves and sherry and braise over low heat for 1 hour, turning twice, until the meat is tender. Remove the duck and keep warm.
5 Add the cabbage to the stock and braise for 20 minutes until half-done. Remove the cabbage and leek, and simmer the remaining braising liquid for 30–45 minutes until it thickens to the consistency of gravy. Slice the duck, and serve with the Stuffing, vegetables and the gravy on the side.

Serves 4   Preparation time: 30 mins   Cooking time: 2 hours

Custard in Meringue   Brazo De Mercedes

A mouth-watering dessert of Spanish origin named after the mysterious Mercedes, who was perhaps the lady responsible for introducing this extravagant dessert to the Philippines.

Softened butter, for brushing

Custard
1 cup (250 ml) sweetened condensed milk
2 tablespoons unsalted butter
1 teaspoon vanilla extract
$1/_2$ cup (125 ml) water
8 egg yolks
$1/_4$ cup (50 g) roasted unsalted cashew nuts, coarsely ground

Meringue
10 egg whites
1 teaspoon cream of tartar
1 cup (125 g) superfine caster sugar
1 teaspoon vanilla extract

1 Combine the condensed milk, butter, vanilla extract and water in a saucepan and simmer over low heat until well combined, about 5 minutes. Beat the egg yolks in a small mixing bowl. Place the mixing bowl over a double boiler over low heat. Gradually pour the milk mixture into the bowl with the yolks, stirring to prevent curdling. Add the cashew nuts and continue to stir over low heat until the mixture has the consistency of a custard. Remove from the heat and set aside.
2 Line a 14 x 16 in (35 x 40 cm) cookie sheet with greased parchment paper and set aside. Preheat the oven to 350°F (180°C). Make the Meringue by beating the egg whites and cream of tartar with an electric mixer in a large mixing bowl. Gradually add the sugar and continue to beat until the Meringue forms stiff peaks. It is important not to overmix the Meringue. Then gently fold in the vanilla extract.
3 Spread the Meringue evenly on the lined cookie sheet to form a $1/_4$-in ($1/_2$-cm) thick layer. Bake in the preheated oven until browned, about 20 minutes or until the Meringue has set.
4 Remove the Meringue from the oven and invert it onto another sheet of greased parchment paper. Peel away the parchment paper on top and spread the Custard evenly on top of the cooked Meringue. Roll it carefully to form a log. Brush the top of the log with a little softened butter and brown again in the oven for 3 to 5 minutes. Remove the log from the oven, slice thinly and serve with tea.

Note: If sweetened condensed milk is not available, substitute with 2 cups (500 ml) evaporated milk or cream simmered with 1 cup (200 g) sugar in a pan until all the sugar is dissolved and the mixture is creamy. Allow the mixture to cool, then proceed with the rest of the recipe. Omit the water in the recipe.

Serves 6–8   Preparation time: 20 mins   Cooking time: 45 mins

Sweet Coconut Corn Cake   Maja Blanca Maiz

2 cups (9 oz/275 g) fresh or frozen
  corn kernels
10 cups (2¹/₂ liters) milk
1 cup (200 g) sugar
1 teaspoon toasted aniseed

Latik
3 cups (750 ml) thick coconut milk

1 Make the Latik by boiling the coconut milk over low heat in a wok, stirring constantly for about an hour until the oil separates, the liquid evaporates and the coconut milk solids fry in the oil to form a crunchy residue, Latik. The cooked mixture should not have any traces of liquid left in it. Remove from the heat and scoop out the Latik with a slotted spoon and drain on paper towels in a cool dish. Strain the coconut oil and set aside.
2 Grease a serving plate with a little coconut oil and set aside. Blend the corn kernels in a food processor with 2 cups (500 ml) of the milk until smooth and strain into a saucepan to remove any remaining lumps or solids. Add the remaining milk and the sugar, and cook over medium heat, stirring constantly until the mixture starts to thicken. Reduce the heat and drizzle in $^1/_2$ cup (125 ml) of the reserved coconut oil and mix well. When the mixture is very thick, add the aniseed and mix well again.
3 Spoon the mixture into the greased serving platter and allow it to cool. Garnish with a sprinkling of the Latik and serve with hot Ginger Tea (page 109).

Note: **Latik** has a delicate, golden yellow color and should not be burnt. Skim the Latik out of the oil quickly into a cool dish to prevent it from turning a darker brown. Latik keeps for a week in a sealed container in the refrigerator.

Serves 6–8   Preparation time: 15 mins   Cooking time: 1 hour 15 mins

Crème Caramel   Leche Flan

5 thin slices lime, to garnish (optional)

Caramel
$^1/_2$ cup (100 g) brown sugar
$^1/_4$ cup (60 ml) water

Custard
12 egg yolks
1 cup (250 ml) fresh milk
One 14-oz (400-g) can sweetened
  condensed milk or 1$^1/_2$ cups (375 ml)
  cream with $^1/_4$ cup (50 g) sugar
1 teaspoon vanilla extract

1 Make the Caramel by boiling the brown sugar and water in a saucepan, stirring continuously over medium heat until the sugar is melted and turns golden brown. Pour the syrup into flan molds or custard cups, or an 8 in (20 cm) diameter baking dish, tilting to make sure the whole surface is covered. Set the mold aside for a minute to allow the Caramel to harden.
2 Preheat the oven to 325°F (160°C). Gently combine all the Custard ingredients in a large bowl, preventing any bubbles or foam from forming. Strain gently into the caramel-lined molds.
3 Cover the molds or baking dish with aluminum foil and place in a bain-marie. Bake in the oven for an hour or until the mixture is firm. Remove from the oven and chill in the refrigerator for 3–4 hours before serving.
4 To serve, run a spatula or knife along the edge of the mold to loosen the Caramel. Turn out onto a serving platter and garnish with lime slices if desired.

Note: When preparing a large Filipino meal, bake the Crème Caramel a day in advance and leave to chill overnight in the refrigerator.

Serves 4–8   Preparation time: 15 mins   Cooking time: 1 hour

Caramel-coated Egg Nuggets Yema

Two wickedly delicious sugar and egg confections from Gene Gonzalez at Cafe Ysabel in Manila.

Egg Nuggets
7 egg yolks
3 whole eggs
$1/4$ cup (60 ml) evaporated milk
  or cream
3 tablespoons sugar (optional)
1 teaspoon vanilla extract

Caramel Coating
$3/4$ cup (150 g) sugar
$1/4$ cup (60 ml) water
$1/4$ teaspoon cream of tartar

1 Make the Egg Nuggets by combining the yolks, whole eggs, milk and sugar, and heating in a double boiler. When the mixture is syrupy, add the vanilla extract and continue to mix for another 10 minutes until the mixture thickens enough to shape into balls. Remove from the heat and set aside to cool. Chill the mixture in the refrigerator for an hour for easier handling.
2 Make the Caramel Coating by heating the sugar, water and cream of tartar in a saucepan stirring constantly until the sugar caramelizes and forms a golden syrup. Keep warm over low heat.
3 Shape about $1/2$ tablespoon of the Egg Nugget mixture into a small ball and dip it into the syrup with a pair of tongs, swirling to coat evenly. Place the coated ball onto a greased pan and set aside to cool. Repeat to form the rest of the Egg Nuggets. Serve cooled in a small bowl or wrap individual Egg Nuggets in colored cellophane paper if desired.

Note: A little mashed boiled sweet potato may be added to the Egg Nugget mixture to thicken it. The prepared Egg Nuggets keep in the refrigerator for up to 2 weeks.

Serves 4   Preparation time: 15 mins   Cooking time: 30 mins

Egg Custard with Caramel Topping Tocino Del Cielo

Caramel Topping
1 cup (200 g) sugar
$1/4$ cup (60 ml) water
1 teaspoon lime or lemon juice

Egg Custard
1 cup (7 oz/200 g) sugar
$1/2$ cup (125 ml) water
2 oz (60 g) butter, softened
12 egg yolks

1 Make the Caramel Topping by combining the sugar, water and lime juice in a saucepan. Bring to a boil and continue to stir until the syrup turns golden brown, about 10 minutes. Pour the caramel syrup into small molds.
2 Preheat the oven to 350°F (180°C). Make the Egg Custard by boiling the sugar and water in a saucepan for 10 to 15 minutes, stirring continuously, until the syrup thickens. Remove from the heat and leave to cool in the saucepan. When cooled, add the butter and egg yolks, and mix well. Strain the mixture through a wire sieve to remove any lumps.
3 Pour the Egg Custard mixture into the caramel-lined molds. Place the molds in a pan with enough water to submerge them halfway. The pan should have sides taller than the molds. Cover the pan with a flat tray and bake for 1 hour, or until a toothpick inserted into the center of a *tocino* comes out clean.
4 Turn off the heat and allow the *tocinos* cool inside the oven. Unmold by running a thin, sharp knife around the edge of each mold. Turn out the *tocinos* onto a plate and serve.

Makes 10–12 *tocinos*   Preparation time: 15 mins   Cooking time: 1 hour 15 mins

Halo Halo Supreme   Exotic Fruit Mix

Known as the "Queen of Desserts"—this is the Philippine's most beloved treat. Similar to Malaysian Ice Kacang, it features exotic fruits and sweets that Filipinos enjoy. This indulgent recipe from Gene Gonzalez at Cafe Ysabel in Manila calls for everything all at once, but you can easily substitute or reduce the number of ingredients to simplify the preparation.

Topping
$^1/_2$ cup (125 ml) pandanus syrup (see note) or maple syrup
$1^1/_2$ cups (375 ml) evaporated milk or fresh cream
4 tablespoons Crème Caramel (page 99)
4 tablespoons *pinipig* or rice crispies
4 scoops French vanilla ice cream

Base
4 teaspoons sweet red adzuki beans (see note)
4 teaspoons sweet yellow mung beans (see note)
4 tablespoons banana or boiled plantain, mashed
4 tablespoons boiled and mashed purple yam (*ube*)
4 tablespoons coconut sport (*macapuno*)
4 tablespoons coconut gelatin (*nata de coco*)
4 tablespoons palm nuts (*kaong*)
4 tablespoons sweet creamed corn
Shaved ice

1 Fill the bottom halves of four serving bowls with the Base ingredients. Cover with shaved ice to reach the top of the bowls.
2 Drizzle the pandanus syrup or maple syrup and milk or cream over each bowl. Top with a tablespoon each of the Crème Caramel and *pinipig*, and a scoop of the ice cream. Serve immediately.

Note: To make **pandanus syrup**, blend 4 pandanus leaves in a food processor with $^1/_4$ cup (60 ml) water, then add 3 tablespoons sugar and heat in a saucepan until it thickens. Strain to remove the bits of pandanus leaves. Pandanus extract is available in bottles in Filipino shops and you can make pandanus syrup by combining $^1/_4$ teaspoon pandanus extract with $^1/_2$ cup (125 ml) sugar syrup. Sweet adzuki beans and mung beans are available in cans. Purple yams and plantains should be rinsed and boiled whole for 20 minutes, then peeled and mashed. Add a bit of sugar if desired. Coconut sport, coconut gelatin and palm nuts are available in bottles.

Serves 4   Preparation time: 20 mins

Sago Pearls with Coconut Gelatin   Sago At Nata De Coco

Traditional desserts from Lito Dalangin at the Villa Escudero. Look for bottles of coconut gelatin (*nata de coco*), palm nuts (*kaong*), young coconut flesh (*buko*) and purple yam pudding in Filipino stores.

1/2 cup (100 g) dried sago pearls
1/2 teaspoon pandanus extract
  or 5 pandanus leaves
1 1/2 cups (375 ml) water
1/2 cup (100 g) sugar
1/2 cup (5 oz/150 g) coconut gelatin
  (*nata de coco*)

Serves 4   Preparation time: 5 mins
Cooking time: 25 mins

1 Rinse the sago pearls and boil in 8 cups (2 liters) water in a pot, stirring constantly for 15 minutes. Cover the pot and set aside for 5 minutes. Then drain, rinse and set the sago pearls aside.
2 Bring the pandanus extract or pandanus leaves and water to a boil. Add the sugar and stir for another 5 minutes. If using pandanus leaves, remove and discard them. Add the drained sago and coconut gelatin and stir continuously for 10 minutes until the mixture is thick and creamy. Keep stirring to keep the ingredients from sticking to the bottom of the pan.
3 Remove from the heat and set aside to cool. Serve well chilled.

Fresh Coconut Delight   Buko Salad

4 tablespoons dried sago pearls
One 15-oz (425-g) can fruit cocktail
One 15-oz (425-g) can sweet corn
  kernels or sweet creamed corn
1/2 cup (5 oz/150 g) sweet coconut
  gelatin (*nata de coco*)
1/2 cup (4 oz/125 g) sweet palm nuts
  (*kaong*)
2 cups (10 oz/300 g) young coconut
  flesh (*buko*)
1/2 cup (125 ml) sweetened condensed milk (see note)
1/2 cup (45 g) grated cheddar cheese
  (optional)

Serves 4   Preparation time: 5 mins

1 Rinse the sago pearls and boil in 4 cups (1 liter) water in a pot, stirring constantly for 15 minutes. Cover the pot and set aside for 5 minutes. Then drain, rinse and set the sago pearls aside.
2 Drain the fruit cocktail, corn kernels, coconut gelatin, palm nuts and young coconut flesh.
3 Toss all the ingredients in a large bowl, then cover and set aside in the refrigerator until required. Serve well chilled.

Note: You may substitute 1/2 cup (125 ml) fresh cream mixed with 1/2 cup (125 ml) of the syrup from the fruit cocktail for the sweetened condensed milk if the latter is not available.

Yam Pudding with Coconut Cream Topping   Crema De Ube

Yam Pudding
1 1/4 lbs (600 g) purple yam (*ube*)
1 cup (250 ml) fresh milk
3/4 cup (150 g) sugar
Macapuno balls (optional)

Topping
1 cup (250 ml) thick coconut milk
1/2 cup (125 ml) water
1/2 cup (125 ml) sweetened condensed milk (see note)
1/2 cup (125 ml) fresh milk
1 tablespoon cornstarch dissolved in
  4 tablespoons water

Serves 4–6   Preparation time: 30 mins
Cooking time: 45 mins

1 To make the Yam Pudding, rinse and boil the yams for 20 to 30 minutes, then peel and grate them. Combine the grated yam with the milk and sugar in a thick-bottomed saucepan. Cook over medium heat until the mixture is very thick, about 15 minutes. Stir constantly to prevent it from sticking to the saucepan. Scoop the pudding into a greased serving bowl or platter. Use the back of a spoon to smooth the surface of the pudding and set aside to cool.
2 Make the Topping by cooking the coconut milk in a saucepan over medium heat for 5 minutes, stirring constantly to avoid scorching. Add the water, condensed milk, fresh milk and the cornstarch mixture, and continue stirring for another 10 minutes until the mixture is creamy. Set aside to cool.
3 To serve, top the Yam Pudding with the Topping and garnish with colorful, sweet *macapuno* balls, if using.

Note: Substitute 1/2 cup (125 ml) whipping cream or evaporated milk mixed with 3 tablespoons sugar for the sweetened condensed milk if the latter is not available. Also omit the cornstarch in the recipe.

Rice Patties with Sweet Grated Coconut   Palitao

2 cups (250 g) glutinous rice flour
1 cup (250 ml) water
3 cups (450 g) freshly grated
   coconut mixed with 2 cups (400 g)
   sugar
Toasted sesame seeds, to garnish
   (optional)

1 In a mixing bowl, knead the rice flour and water to make a smooth dough that holds together and separates cleanly from the pan. With floured hands, pinch off about 1$^1/_2$ tablespoons of the dough and shape into a small patty, about 2 in (5 cm) in diameter and about $^1/_2$ in (1 cm) thick. Set aside on a dry plate. Repeat with the rest of the dough to make about 30 patties in all.
2 Place the sweetened coconut into a bowl. Drop the patties into a saucepan of boiling water. When they float to the top, scoop them out with a slotted spoon, drain and place into the bowl with the coconut. Garnish with sesame seeds, if using, and serve hot or at room temperature.

Serves 6–8   Preparation time: 10 mins   Cooking time: 15 mins

Brown Rice Flour Cakes   Kutsinta

2 cups (250 g) rice flour
1$^1/_2$ cups (300 g) brown sugar
3 cups (750 ml) water
1 teaspoon lye water (potassium carbonate solution)
Freshly grated coconut, dry-fried in a
   skillet over low heat until golden
   brown, or Latik (page 99), to garnish

1 Mix the rice flour, sugar, water and lye water in a bowl. Spoon the mixture into small muffin pans until about halfway full.
2 Steam in a large, covered pan for 30 minutes or until a toothpick inserted into the rice cakes comes out clean. Add more water to the pan if needed until the rice cakes are firm and fully cooked.
3 Remove the rice cakes from the molds by running a sharp knife around the edges of the molds. Garnish with crispy roasted coconut and serve hot or at room temperature.

Serves 4–6   Preparation time: 15 mins   Cooking time: 1 hour 30 mins

Cassava Patties with Coconut   Pichi-Pichi

$^1/_2$ cup (125 ml) pandanus water or
   $^1/_4$ teaspoon pandanus extract
   mixed with $^1/_2$ cup (125 ml) water
1 cup (225 g) grated cassava
$^1/_4$ cup (50 g) sugar
1 teaspoon lye water (potassium carbonate solution)
1 cup (150 g) freshly grated coconut

1 To make pandanus water, blend 10 pandanus leaves with 1 cup (250 ml) water in a blender or food processor and strain the liquid.
2 Mix the cassava, sugar, pandanus water and lye water in a bowl until the sugar is completely dissolved. Shape the mixture into patties about 3 in (8 cm) in diameter and $^1/_2$ in (1 cm) thick. Line the top rack of a steamer with banana leaves. Steam the patties for 45 minutes, or until firm, then remove from the steamer and set aside to cool.
3 When cool enough to handle, but still warm, roll the cooked patties in the grated coconut and serve.

Note: **Pandanus water** imparts a delicate fragrance and a green hue to desserts. To make pandanus water, blend 10 pandanus leaves with 1 cup (250 ml) water in a blender or food processor and strain the liquid. Cassava is often grated and used to prepare cakes and snacks. Frozen cassava is available in some Asian food stores.

Serves 4–6   Preparation time: 20 mins   Cooking time: 45 mins

Lemongrass Pandanus Iced Tea

30 pandanus leaves or 2 tablespoons
  McCormick Pandan Extract
5 stalks lemongrass, bruised
$^1/_2$-$^3/_4$ cup (100-150 g) sugar
12 cups (3 liters) water

1 In a large pot, boil the pandanus leaves, lemongrass and sugar in the water until the liquid is reduced to half, about 30 minutes. Strain and discard the solids.
2 Set the pandanus-infused tea aside to cool. Serve with ice in tall glasses.

Serves 5   Preparation time: 20 mins   Cooking time: 30 mins

Ginger Tea   Salabat

8 oz (250 g) fresh ginger, peeled,
  sliced into chunks and bruised
5 cups (1$^1/_4$ liters) water
$^1/_2$-1 cup (100-150 g) brown sugar

1 Boil all the ingredients in a pot for 30 minutes. Add more water if the tea is too strong. Strain and serve hot or chilled.

Serves 4–5   Preparation time: 15 mins   Cooking time: 30 mins

Green Mango Shake

$^1/_4$ cup (50 g) sugar or 4 tablespoons
  honey
$^1/_2$ cup (125 ml) hot water
2 unripe mangoes, peeled and pitted,
  flesh cubed
2 cups crushed ice

1 Dissolve the sugar or honey in the hot water and set aside.
2 Blend the mangoes with the syrup and crushed ice in a blender at medium speed. Gradually increase the blending speed until the mixture is creamy and the ice is finely ground. Serve immediately.

Serves 2   Preparation time: 10 mins

Fresh Mango Shake

2 ripe mangoes
3 cups crushed ice
Sugar (optional)

1 Peel the mangoes and, using a knife, scrape off the flesh from the seed. Pulp the flesh in a processor, then add the crushed ice and blend at medium speed to mix well, to form a thick, creamy shake.
2 Add sugar to taste and serve in tall glasses immediately.

Serves 2   Preparation time: 5 mins

Measurements and conversions

Measurements in this book are given in volume as far as possible. Teaspoon, tablespoon and cup measurements should be level, not heaped, unless otherwise indicated. Australian readers please note that the standard Australian measuring spoon is larger than the UK or American spoon by 5 ml, so use $3/4$ tablespoon instead of a full tablespoon when following the recipes.

Liquid Conversions

Imperial	Metric	US cups
$1/2$ fl oz	15 ml	1 tablespoon
1 fl oz	30 ml	$1/8$ cup
2 fl oz	60 ml	$1/4$ cup
3 fl oz	85 ml	$1/3$ cup
4 fl oz	125 ml	$1/2$ cup
5 fl oz	150 ml	$2/3$ cup
6 fl oz	175 ml	$3/4$ cup
8 fl oz	250 ml	1 cup
12 fl oz	375 ml	$1 1/2$ cups
16 fl oz	500 ml	2 cups
1 quart	1 liter	4 cups

Note:
1 UK pint = 20 fl oz
1 US pint = 16 fl oz

Solid Weight Conversions

Imperial	Metric
$1/2$ oz	15 g
1 oz	28 g
$1 1/2$ oz	45 g
2 oz	60 g
3 oz	85 g
$3 1/2$ oz	100 g
4 oz ($1/4$ lb)	125 g
5 oz	150 g
6 oz	175 g
7 oz	200 g
8 oz ($1/2$ lb)	225 g
9 oz	260 g
10 oz	300 g
16 oz (1 lb)	450 g
32 oz (2 lbs)	1 kg

Oven Temperatures

Heat	Fahrenheit	Centigrade/Celsius	British Gas Mark
Very cool	230	110	$1/4$
Cool or slow	275–300	135–150	1–2
Moderate	350	175	4
Hot	425	220	7
Very hot	450	230	8

Index of recipes

Mail-order/online sources

The ingredients used in this book can all be found in markets featuring the foods of Southeast Asia. Many of them can also be found in any well-stocked supermarket. Ingredients not found locally may be available from the mail-order/online addresses listed below.

Asiana Market
www.asianamarket.com

Asian Grocer
33 East Main Street
Buckhannon West Virginia 26201
Tel: 304-473-1444

Bangkok-Manila Grocery
30-81 31
Astoria New York
Tel:(718) 956-9811

Central Market
4001 N Lamar Blvd.
Austin, Texas
Tel: 512-206-1000
www.centralmarket.com

Mabuhay Asian Groceries and Gifts
901-B Pine Tree Rd
Longview TX 75604
Tel: (903) 291-8899
www.mabuhaygrocery.com

Manila Mart
6051 Martin Luther King, Jr. Way
Seattle WA 98118-3141
Tel:(206) 723-8656

Manila Supermarket
3901 W Fm 196 Rd
Houston Texas
Tel: (713) 397-8747

Nipa Hut Oriental Market
5447 S. Rainbow Blvd
Suite E-2 Las Vegas, NV 89118
Tel: 702 248 NIPA(6472)
www.nipahutorientalmarket.com

Pacific Filipino Oriental Store
2254 Pacific Ave
Long Beach California 90806-4312
Tel: (562) 591-7599

Philippine Grocery
5750 N California Ave
Chicago Illinois 60659-4726
Tel: (312) 334-4628

Philippine Asian Supermarket
5430 North Tryon St. Ste. 1
Charlotte North Carolina 28213
Tel: 704-921-0703
Amelia12668@aol.com

Philippine Oriental Foods
3611 NE 82nd Ave
Portland Oregon 97220-5121
Tel: (503) 331-6950

Phil Thai Grocers
29-24 36 Ave
Long Island New York 11106-3108
Tel:(718) 392-5512

PilipinoMart
2422 W Temple St.
Los Angeles, CA 90026
Fax: (703) 995-4582 (Virginia)
       (213) 947-1314 (California)
info@pilipinomart.com.

Pinoy Store
28 Little Mary Street Dublin 7 Ireland
Phone: 87-801167
Owner: Siony Alteza

Thai Philippine Oriental Foods
523 Gorsuch Ave
Baltimore Maryland 21218-3550
Tel: (410) 243-6193

The Philippine Market
5751 Old Hickory Blvd. Suite 108
Hermitage Tennesse 37076
Tel: 615-874-0067
philmarket@aol.com

Perlas Limited
3-5 Stanhope Road
South Shields, Tyne and Wear
NE 33 4BA UK
Tel: (44) 0191-454-2000
www.orientalfoodsupplies.co.uk

Philipines Asian Grocery
5 Floristan Road (shop 6)
Boronia, Melbourne
Australia